LA CORT D'AMOR
A CRITICAL EDITION

THE EUROPEAN HUMANITIES RESEARCH CENTRE

UNIVERSITY OF OXFORD

The European Humanities Research Centre of the University of Oxford organizes a range of academic activities, including conferences and workshops, and publishes scholarly works under its own imprint, LEGENDA. Within Oxford, the EHRC bridges, at the research level, the main Humanities faculties: Modern Languages, English, Modern History, Classics and Philosophy, and Music and Theology. The Centre facilitates interdisciplinary research collaboration throughout these subject areas and provides an Oxford base for advanced researchers in the Humanities.

The Centre's publications programme focuses on making available the results of advanced research in medieval and modern languages and related interdisciplinary areas. An Editorial Board, whose members are drawn from across the British university system, covers the principal European languages and literatures. The LEGENDA list currently includes works on Arabic, Catalan, Chinese, English, French, German, Italian, Portuguese, Russian, Spanish and Yiddish literature. In addition, the EHRC co-publishes with the Society for French Studies, the Modern Humanities Research Association and the British Comparative Literature Association. The Centre publishes a Special Lecture Series under the Legenda imprint, and the journal *Oxford German Studies*.

Enquiries about the Centre's publishing activities should be addressed to:
Professor Malcolm Bowie, Director

Editorial Coordinator for French
Dr Nicola Luckhurst, Somerville College

Further information:
Kareni Bannister, Senior Publications Officer
European Humanities Research Centre
University of Oxford
47 Wellington Square, Oxford OX1 2JF
enquiries@ehrc.ox.ac.uk
www.ehrc.ox.ac.uk

LEGENDA

RESEARCH MONOGRAPHS IN FRENCH STUDIES

Editorial Committee
Professor Michael Moriarty, Queen Mary & Westfield College, London
(General Editor)
Dr Adrian Armstrong, University of Manchester
Dr Wendy Ayres-Bennett, New Hall, Cambridge
Professor Celia Britton, University of Aberdeen
Professor Diana Knight, University of Nottingham
Professor Bill Marshall, University of Glasgow

❖

Published in this series:
1. *Privileged Anonymity: The Writings of Madame de Lafayette*
by Anne Green
2. *Stéphane Mallarmé. Correspondance: compléments et suppléments*
edited by Lloyd James Austin, Bertrand Marchal and Nicola Luckhurst
3. *Critical Fictions: Nerval's 'Les Illuminés'*
by Meryl Tyers
4. *Towards a Cultural Philology:* Phèdre *and the Construction of 'Racine'*
by Amy Wygant
5. *George Sand and Autobiography*
by Janet Hiddleston
6. *Expressivism: The Vicissitudes of a Theory in the Writing of
Proust and Barthes*, by Johnnie Gratton
7. *Memory and Survival: The French Cinema of Krzysztof Kieślowski*
by Emma Wilson
8. *Between Sequence and* Sirventes: *Aspects of Parody in the Troubadour Lyric*
by Catherine Léglu
9. *All Puns Intended: The Verbal Creation of Jean-Pierre Brisset*
by Walter Redfern
10. *Saint-Evremond: A Voice From Exile*
by Denys Potts

LEGENDA

European Humanities Research Centre
Research Monographs in French Studies 11

La Cort d'Amor
A Critical Edition

❖

Matthew Bardell

LEGENDA

European Humanities Research Centre
University of Oxford
Research Monographs in French Studies 11
2002

Published for the Society for French Studies by the
European Humanities Research Centre
of the University of Oxford
47 Wellington Square
Oxford OX1 2JF

LEGENDA is the publications imprint of the
European Humanities Research Centre

ISBN 1 900755 66 1
ISSN 1466–8157

First published 2002

All rights reserved. No part of this publication may be reproduced or disseminated or transmitted in any form or by any means, electronic, mechanical, photocopying, recording or otherwise, or stored in any retrieval system, or otherwise used in any manner whatsoever without the express permission of the copyright owner

British Library Cataloguing in Publication Data
A CIP catalogue record for this book is available from the British Library

© *European Humanities Research Centre of the University of Oxford 2002*

LEGENDA series designed by Cox Design Partnership, Witney, Oxon
Printed in Great Britain by
Information Press
Eynsham
Oxford OX8 1JJ

Chief Copy-Editor: Genevieve Hawkins

CONTENTS

❖

Acknowledgements	ix
Abbreviations	x
Introduction	1
Editorial Principles	34
Edition and translation of the *Cort d'Amor*	41
Notes	136
Glossary	159
Bibliography	163
Index	168

ACKNOWLEDGEMENTS
❖

This edition of the *Cort d'Amor* first began to take shape as a one-year project for an MA by research at the University of Warwick. Working on this fascinating text gave me an appetite for medieval allegory, and led me to undertake doctoral research on secular narrative allegory. Vernacular allegories prior to the *Roman de la Rose* have been surprisingly neglected by modern scholars and in the case of the *Cort d'Amor* this is in no small part due to the lack of a readily available and reliable edition. I therefore resolved to dust off my dissertation, thoroughly revise the edition itself, and write a new introduction in light of my doctoral research. The current edition is thus the culmination of six years' work on and around the *Cort d'Amor*. During that time I have had the good fortune to benefit from the support of a number of people and organizations, and it a great pleasure to be able to thank them here.

First and foremost I should like to thank Linda Paterson, without whom I should never have undertaken the edition in the first place. Having proposed the project to me, Linda supervised my MA and has since continued to suggest improvements as the revision has progressed. Although any remaining imperfections are naturally my responsibility, Linda is to be thanked for a great deal of what is good in the edition. I should also like to thank the Paul Hamlyn Foundation for providing me with the grant which made my year at Warwick possible, and Carol, Gill, Emmanuel, Jason and Toby, who made that year a memorable one.

In the preparation and revision of the edition, I have also gratefully received help and advice on numerous points of detail from Peter Davies, Peter Dronke, Sarah Kay, Peter Noble, Mike Routledge and the anonymous reader for French Studies Monographs. I should like to thank Michael Moriarty for agreeing to publish this edition in the French Studies Monographs Series, and Kareni Bannister and Graham Nelson at the European Humanities Research Centre for preparing and producing the typescript. Finally, I should like to thank my parents for their constant interest, encouragement and support throughout the preparation of this edition. It is to them that I dedicate it.

ABBREVIATIONS

❖

Anglade   Joseph Anglade, *Grammaire de l'ancien provençal ou ancienne langue d'oc: Phonétique et morphologie* (Paris: Klincksieck, 1921).

FEW   Walther von Wartburg, *Französisches etymologisches Wörterbuch: Eine Darstellung des galloromanischen Sprachsetzes*, 22 vols., 3 supplements and 15 unbound parts (new edn. Tübingen: Mohr, 1948–83).

Jensen   Frede Jensen, *Syntaxe de l'ancien occitan*, Beihefte zur Zeitschrift für romanische Philologie 257 (Tübingen: Niemeyer, 1994). References to this work are by page numbers, not sigla.

PD   Emil Levy, *Petit Dictionnaire provençal-français* (Heidelberg: Winter, 1909).

PSW   Emil Levy, *Provenzalisches Supplement-Wörterbuch*, 8 vols. (Leipzig: Reisland, 1894–1924).

Raynouard   François Raynouard, *Lexique roman; ou, Dictionnaire de la langue des troubadours*, 5 vols. (Paris: Silvestre, 1838–45).

In the Notes, references to **Bartsch**, **Chabaneau**, **Constans**, **Jones**, **Levy** and **Mahn** refer to their editions/corrections of the *Cort d'Amor* cited in the Bibliography. (Nelli and Lavaud simply reproduce their excerpt from Constans's 1881 edition, and so are not mentioned.) Unless otherwise stated, references to Constans are to his revised 1882 edition. Where I refer to one of Levy's dictionaries, I omit his name and simply use the above abbreviation for the dictionary in question.

INTRODUCTION

❖

Manuscript and Date

The *Cort d'Amor* (incipit: [S]*einor, vos que volez la flor*) is preserved solely in Occitan Chansonnier N, now MS M.819 in the Pierpont Morgan Library, New York City.[1] The work is anonymous and makes no direct reference to contemporary events or figures which might give clues as to when it was written. Nor are any direct allusions to this poem to be found in any other contemporary or near-contemporary writing. The manuscript itself is therefore the first point of reference in any attempt to date the text. Whilst the more recent history of Chansonnier N has been firmly established,[2] little is known of its history prior to 1816 apart from the fact that it belonged to the Gonzagas, Dukes of Mantua, between 1384 and the early sixteenth century at least. It came into their possession upon the execution of Andrea Painelli, who had inherited the manuscript from his father, Giacomino. The presence of the act granting Giacomino Painelli and his descendants citizenship of Mantua, dated 1354, at folio 53^v, possibly led some scholars to date the entire manuscript as fourteenth-century.[3] However, Giuseppe Frasso, albeit identifying the script as fourteenth-century, points out that in all probability Giacomino Painelli had the act *inserted* into his favourite manuscript.[4]

Studies on the illustrations of Chansonnier N, however, propose an earlier date. Meta Harrsen and George K. Boyce identify the illustrations as late thirteenth-century and of Paduan provenance—'Ms. in vellum, written and illuminated at Padua, Italy, at the end of the thirteenth century with miniatures by an artist of the atelier of Giovanni Gaibana'[5]—but this assumption is refuted by Gianfranco Folena, who points out that Giovanni Gaibana was in fact a scribe, not a miniaturist.[6] Folena goes on to date the script as mid-thirteenth-century, although 'le illustrazioni sono certo assai più tarde', and situates the place of production somewhere in the area between Mantua and Padua. D'Arco Silvio Avalle counters the Paduan association of Harrsen and Boyce, judging that the similarities they found between N and the Epistles of 1259 preserved in Padua Cathedral 'non sono dei più evidenti'; rather, the technique of portraying figures and isolating them from the rest of the page is more similar to the *Sermone* of Pietro da Bescapé (Milan, thirteenth-century).[7] Bernhard Degenhart and Annegrit Schmitt place the production of the manuscript in Venice or Padua in the second half of the thirteenth century,[8] whilst François Avril and M. T. Gousset comment that the extent of reciprocal influence between these two great centres makes it impossible to distinguish between the two, given the current state of knowledge.[9] Roger Sherman Loomis and Laura Hibbard Loomis describe the extension of letters into lancets curving into leaves (recurrent throughout N) as 'one of the most characteristic motifs of north Italian, and particularly Bolognese, decoration in the last half of the thirteenth century and the first half of the fourteenth'.[10]

Finally, in her edition of the *Cort d'Amor*, Lowanne E. Jones cites an unpublished Pierpont Morgan Library file on the manuscript: 'The date of M.819 can be fixed between 1285 and 1300 by certain details of costumes, iconography and calligraphic ornament. Among these are the types of costumes, the fillet worn by the women on their brows, the chain armor and shields, the shape of the bishop's mitre (f. 55); the type of filigrane ornament, and the modelling and posture of Christ on the cross in folio f. 65. These are all before 1300.'[11] In the absence of more substantial justification of these points, the fact that Jones cites the file as still attributing the miniatures to Gaibana's atelier suggests that the precision of its dating is open to question.

With so many differing opinions and observations, few of which seem to be fully justified beyond the occasional claim of similarity with datable models, it seems prudent to conclude with Avalle that a close study of miniatures produced both in Italy and the other side of the Alps would be necessary to make a definitive judgement. One might perhaps note that the fourteenth/fifteenth-century assumption of earlier critics (Suchier, Brunel, Pillet, Jeanroy) has been abandoned in favour of a mid/late-thirteenth-century date in more recent commentaries. Whilst the manuscript tradition thus does not tell us very much about the date of composition of our text, it seems prudent to assume a date of composition not later than the end of the thirteenth century.

If this is our *terminus ante quem*, how long before that could the *Cort d'Amor* have been written? Is there any evidence of distinct intertextuality with other works which would help us to situate it in time?

Jones gives a list of 'borrowings' from other troubadours from the very end of the twelfth century and the start of the thirteenth (pp. 47–8), but when she cites the specific passages in question (in a section entitled 'Notes to the Translation', pp. 209–22) it becomes clear that it is merely a question of commonplaces shared with the lyric tradition. Jones also traces individual features of the work, such as the garden of Love, in Latin, Old French and Occitan literature, but whilst the *Cort d'Amor* certainly fits into such a tradition, she is unable to demonstrate any direct textual influence. Ernest Langlois, writing almost ninety years earlier, had attributed such features in similar texts to common sources.[12] Jones postulates a date of composition not earlier than the first decade of the thirteenth century on the basis of her exploration of 'borrowings'. Given the longevity of the commonplaces in question, however, it would be very difficult to place the *Cort d'Amor* so accurately in time. Although the stylistic features are consistent with the date she proposes, they would not be out of place in a work from any time between the 1180s and the 1270s.

Jones follows the *Cort d'Amor*'s first editor, Léopold Constans,[13] in asserting a date of composition earlier than Guillaume de Lorris' part of the *Roman de la Rose*, on the basis that it demonstrates no influence from Guillaume de Lorris' work. Although I too think that the Occitan poem is earlier than the Old French one (see below), I cannot concur with the reasoning behind their assertion. For one thing, it assumes a wide circulation of Guillaume's text prior to Jean de Meun's continuation. Whilst Langlois,[14] supported by Sylvia Huot in this respect,[15] claims that the existence of manuscripts containing only the first part of the *Roman de la Rose* demonstrates circulation prior to Jean de Meun, David Hult points out that only two of 250 *Roman de la Rose* manuscripts attest to the prior existence of Guillaume's section,[16] suggesting on the contrary very little circulation before the continuation was written, let alone circulation in Occitania. For another thing, it seems to me to be perverse to assume that no one *could* write a narrative allegory after Guillaume de Lorris without including textual borrowings from him.

Whatever credence is given to the possibility of the early dissemination of Guillaume de Lorris' masterpiece, there are good reasons for supposing that the *Cort d'Amor* enjoyed some kind of circulation in northern France. Whilst Jones concentrates on the Italian features of the orthography, which are most likely attributable to an Italian scribe, given what we know about the early history and illustration of the

4 INTRODUCTION

manuscript, she does not devote any attention to the number of gallicisms in the text. Suchier, however, points out that: 'alcune parti del ms. (specialmente V [our poem], XXXII–XXXV, XLVI) mostrano delle forme che solo un menante francese potè introdurre; esse derivano da un codice scritto in Francia (se direttamente o indirettamente lascio si domandi).'[17] Suchier does not identify specifically what forms he is referring to, but I have compiled a list of gallicisms in the *Cort d'Amor* below (see Part 2 of the Glossary). Whereas many of them could simply be attributed to a French scribe carelessly incorporating northern features whilst copying a text (such as the five instances of final *-nt* for third-person plural verb forms),[18] others suggest a more fundamental influence of French, in particular the presence of gallicisms at the rhyme (ll. 54, 166, 359, 950, 1253, 1622). The evidence thus suggests that the Italian scribes of N had written sources before them, amongst which was at least one of French provenance.[19] This French source was at some stage written by someone with thought if not with consistency. The presence of *el* as a third-person feminine pronoun suggests a Frenchman who was paying enough attention to the text to see that a feminine form was required, even if elsewhere he remembered that the Occitan feminine form was *il*, or simply copied it without reflection.

Although the gallicisms may be described as a significant feature of our text, it is nevertheless written in correct and elegant Occitan. We do not know a great deal about the circulation of poets and texts in and between northern France and Occitania, but it is known that some troubadours performed at northern courts such as the Plantagenet court in England, or that of Marie de Champagne. That our only copy of an Occitan text shows evidence of circulation in northern France is perhaps a sign of generic interest. Certainly more narrative allegories have come down to us in Old French than in Occitan, which boasts very few narrative texts of any kind.[20] The circulation of the *Cort d'Amor* in northern France takes on added significance through the fact that a number of factors link the *Cort d'Amor* with the *De amore* of Andreas Capellanus, also associated with the court of Champagne. I shall deal with these factors in detail below in my discussion of the text itself, as taken individually none is conclusive. Taken collectively, however, I believe they constitute a very strong suggestion that the *Cort d'Amor* was written as a response in kind to Andreas Capellanus' magnum opus and, moreover, that the Occitan work was composed soon after the Latin one. A date of composition at the end of the twelfth century is perfectly concordant with what we know about the manuscript tradition and style of the *Cort d'Amor*.

A *Cort d'Amor* written for the court of Champagne at the end of the twelfth century takes up a very different place in literary history from that which it has hitherto enjoyed. Although it is futile to try and demonstrate intertextuality between our text and Guillaume de Lorris' *Roman de la Rose* beyond those commonplaces of allegorical narratives examined by Langlois (see above), we can hardly ignore the fact that the first vernacular narrative personification allegory which has survived was around in northern France about fifty years before Guillaume de Lorris (accepting Jean de Meun's dating of the latter). The *Cort d'Amor* can, indeed, claim to be the first allegorical romance, given its clear self-styling as a *roman* (cf. ll. 5, 10, 13, 16, and my discussion, below). Although the precise dating and any links with Andreas Capellanus remain speculative, I believe that modern scholars might have paid more attention to the *Cort d'Amor* if such a date and such a link had been seriously proposed and the text's gallicisms had been highlighted.

Modern Reception

If the medieval transmission of the *Cort d'Amor* is riddled with problems, the same can be said of its fate in more recent times. Despite the production of two complete editions of the poem, and the presentation of lengthy sections in three anthologies, a brief survey of the very few studies to examine it will quickly demonstrate how many uncertainties remain over such basic issues as the gender of the major personifications and even how many characters there are.

Although François Raynouard was familiar with the *Cort d'Amor*, discussing *idesa* in his dictionary (see the note to l. 50 below), the first publication of any extract was that of Karl Bartsch in 1855.[21] Bartsch published ll. 1–182, 345–484 and 505–15 on the basis of a copy of those lines from the manuscript made by C. A. F. Mahn, and cited Mahn as his source.[22] Mahn evidently did not tell Bartsch that he had not copied the last two extracts continuously, as Bartsch runs ll. 484 and 505 together. Mahn published the same lines as Bartsch as a diplomatic text a year later, in 1856.[23]

The first complete edition was produced by Constans in 1881.[24] He had travelled to Cheltenham to look at Chansonnier N, at that time in the collection of Sir Thomas Phillips, but he evidently did not have the time to check his readings as there are numerous mistakes in the text he published. It was Constans who first gave this work without title the name 'Cour d'Amour'. Corrections to Constans's edition were proposed by Camille Chabaneau and Emil Levy the following year.[25] Constans published a revised version of his edition in 1882,[26] which is sadly now more difficult to obtain than a copy of the original manuscript, as the latter, like many manuscripts, is now happily available on microfilm in most major research libraries. The Bibliothèque nationale in Paris has a copy of Constans's offprint, and has taken the wise precaution of copying it onto microfiche. The 1882 revision is a considerable improvement on Constans's first attempt, incorporating revisions proposed by Chabaneau (which do not always correspond exactly to the emendations proposed by Chabaneau actually published in the *Revue des langues romanes*—see the note to l. 906, below), comparison with Mahn's reading (which he had not consulted before his first edition) and a thorough review of everything, correcting numerous points of detail. This is what he has to say on the task of editing the *Cort d'Amor* (and other texts from the same manuscript) in 1882:

Le texte du Chansonnier Mac-Carthy, quoique bien peint, offre d'assez grandes difficultés aux éditeurs, non-seulement [sic] à cause des fautes graves qui s'y rencontrent, comme dans la plupart des Chansonniers, mais surtout à cause de la façon plus que fantaisiste dont les mots et les syllabes y sont séparés ou réunis. D'ailleurs, quelques-unes des pièces que nous publions appartiennent au genre *obscur*, et il est quelquefois difficile d'y trouver un sens acceptable, sans trop faire violence aux règles de la paléographie et au texte réel du manuscrit. Nous avons, du reste, marqué d'un point d'interrogation les mots ou vers où nous ne trouvions aucun sens convenable, et nous les livrons aux méditations des provençalistes. (p. 49)

As will be seen shortly when I turn to the critical reception of the *Cort d'Amor*, these *méditations* have been far from uniform, and this is partly due to the dissemination of Constans's less accurate 1881 edition. René Nelli and René Lavaud, publishing ll. 1159–1257 in 1966, merely reproduce that passage from Constans's 1881 edition.[27] Jones, with the second edition of the whole text, inaccurately describes Constans's revision as 'corrected to a small degree' and, with perhaps more justification, 'no longer obtainable' (p. 15).

Jones produced not only a new edition, but also the first translation (into English) of the *Cort d'Amor*. She provides a largely accurate diplomatic edition with a facing translation frequently based on corrections proposed by Constans, Chabaneau, Levy and Bartsch; these corrections are buried in the footnotes and not acknowledged as the basis for her translation. The translation itself is full of mistakes, which leads to much of her critical comment on the text being misinformed. Linda Paterson, reviewing Jones's edition, comments that 'unhappily, the edition represents the well-intentioned work of a student lacking specialist guidance or a critical publisher. The translation teems with mistakes [...] threatening to mislead non-specialists. Linguistic inadequacy confuses argument [...] or makes nonsense of it.'[28] Thus despite the attentions of eight scholars, the *Cort d'Amor* has never been available to the literary critic in a reliable edition, with the best attempt, Constans's revised edition, being virtually unobtainable.

This lack of a readily available and reliable critical edition has led to the *Cort d'Amor* being largely ignored, and in equal measure misunderstood, by critics. Constans and Jones are virtually the only critical voices to express enthusiasm about the text. It is a shame that Constans never found the time to publish what he thought of it. In his revised edition, he describes it as a 'nouvelle fort intéressante' and then goes further:

Nous croyons devoir donner une place à part [...] à une pièce du Chansonnier Mac-Carthy, malheureusement incomplète à la fin, qui mérite toute l'attention des provençalistes, autant par son étendue que par l'intérêt du sujet traité. Cette espèce d'*Art d'aimer* est certainement antérieure au *Roman de la Rose*, et peut fournir matière à une comparaison intéressante avec la partie de cette curieuse composition qui est due à Guillaume de Lorris. On la comparera aussi utilement avec le *Songe vert*, poème français que nous nous proposons de publier incessamment d'après le manuscrit unique de Spalding (Angleterre), ce qui nous fournira l'occasion de revenir sur le poëme provençal. (p. 66)

Unfortunately, it took Constans twenty-two years to eventually publish the *Songe vert*, having been sidetracked by the massive task of editing the *Roman de Thèbes*, and when he did, he noticed that the *Songe vert* has only superficial similarities with the *Cort d'Amor* and so never did develop his ideas on the Occitan text.[29]

Constans's edition did not provoke a great deal of critical comment either, with William Allan Neilson probably being the first to mention it, nearly twenty years later, in his study on texts featuring courts of love; he does little more than list the basic elements of the court.[30] Albert Stimming groups the work with others aiming to improve readers rather than teach them, and describes Amor as 'als Fürstin auf dem Parnasse thronend eingeführt'.[31] This notion of Amor as female in our text was to remain a common one, with Jones reaching the same conclusion. The confusion is caused by l. 30, which speaks of *Amors la dousa e la bona*, but in every other respect Amor is consistently male in our text (on which see my discussion of personification gender, below). Alice Adèle Hentsch similarly saw Amor as a princess, with Fin'Amor as a separate character, and peculiarly claims that 'le poète s'adresse aux femmes mariées de condition noble et incidemment aussi aux jeunes filles nobles' (presumably on the basis of a misreading of ll. 21–5?).[32] Amos Parducci followed Hentsch's account without realizing that she had only summarized the parts of the work constituting advice to ladies, remarking on a similarity in material with the *ensenhamen* of Amenieu de Sescas and on the originality of the use of allegory in an Occitan work, although not elaborating thereon.[33]

Erich Müller was the first to consider the *Cort d'Amor* at any length, in his study of verse narrative forms.[34] Although paying tribute to the wealth of traditions from which the work draws, such as secular allegory in both the vernacular and Latin, and the watchman motif from the *alba*, he described the allegorical narrative as 'farblos gezeichnet' and concluded that the narrative elements were unfortunately subservient to the didactic ones: 'Gerade unser gedicht beweist schlagend, daß die Provenzalen wohl fähig waren, auch in der erzählenden poesie etwas zu leisten. Leider sahen und suchten sie ihren ruhm nur in der didaktik; die erzählung als solche galt ihnen nichts oder nicht viel' (p. 108). Müller did, however, identify Amor as a male personification and saw the target audience as being male (presumably on the basis of [S]*einor* in l. 1).

Marc-René Jung similarly bemoaned the sparseness of the allegory in comparison with the direct speech of the personifications, concluding that 'en tant que poème allégorique, la *Cour d'Amour* est un squelette'.[35] He proposed that the lost ending to the work must have contained a psychomachia, correcting Constans's curious assertion that *Anseis qe movatz* (l. 1651) indicated the imminent close of the work.[36] Jung did not, in the final analysis, consider the *Cort d'Amor* to be a fully allegorical text, calling the personifications *abstracta loquens*, their speeches not always closely identifiable with the notions they represent.

The introduction to Jones's edition is the only study to devote itself wholly to the *Cort d'Amor*. The other critics so far mentioned were only interested in fitting the work into various traditions wherein their real interest lay. However, although our text does have important points of contact with other allegorical and didactic texts, it is unique and deserves to be read for what it is before points of comparison can usefully be made. Unfortunately, as mentioned above, Jones's miscomprehension distorted her arguments, and she claimed that Amor is female and that Cortesa d'Amor and Corteszia are one and the same character. She also had an uninspired approach to literary context, tracing individual elements such as the fountain through other texts without really inquiring what purpose their presence might serve, and listing common images from the lyric tradition without questioning in which direction any influence might be shown to have worked.

Although writing some four years after Jones, Don A. Monson appeared unaware of her edition in his consideration of the *ensenhamens*.[37] If the *Cort d'Amor* was too didactic for Müller and Jung, it was too allegorical for Monson: 'ces *ensenhamens* diffèrent des allégories par le fait que le didactisme des premiers se présente de façon directe, tandis qu'il est de l'essence des secondes de présenter un décalage entre la *lettre* et le *sens*' (p. 95). He then apparently undermined his own position by claiming that in our text 'cette action n'a aucune valeur symbolique: elle n'a d'autre fonction que de fournir un cadre pour les discours des personifications' (pp. 95–6). Monson is certainly correct in separating the dialogic style of the *Cort d'Amor* from the unequivocal didacticism of the *ensenhamens*. As I shall soon demonstrate, he was, along with all other critics who have discussed this text, incorrect in his dismissal of its allegorical status.

It should be clear from this survey that, with the exception of Jones, very little ink has been spilt on the subject of the *Cort d'Amor*.[38] Its existence is acknowledged in *Grundrisse* and occasionally cited in passing in footnotes, but remains largely ignored and frequently maligned. In his overview of Occitan literature, Alfred Jeanroy dismissed it as 'une sorte d'Art d'aimer aussi insipide que décousu'.[39] Robert Lafont and Christian Anatole concurred with Jeanroy on the first count, but not on the second: '[Ce] texte est froid, ennuyeux, mais il faut reconnaître que la langue est d'une grande élégance'.[40] Yet some scholars, like Constans, have recognized something more interesting: Giuseppe E. Sansone, for instance, speaks of it as a 'testo non ancora valutato come meriterebbe'.[41] This text *does* merit the attention of scholars, and not just Occitanists, but also anyone interested in courtly love and medieval allegory.

As Müller pointed out, the *Cort d'Amor* is rich in the number of traditions and genres with which it engages, and I cannot hope to develop fully all such lines of inquiry here. For the remainder of this introduction, however, I propose to point out some rich avenues of investigation for fellow medievalists, and in particular to examine the two major elements of the text: the dialogic didacticism of the Court of Love, and the troubled allegorical narrative. First, however, I provide a synopsis of the whole work, or at least that part which has survived. For the convenience of non-Occitanists, I here translate the names of the personifications into English. Elsewhere in this introduction I retain the Occitan forms.

Synopsis

1–34: Introduction, the didactic aim of the work is expressed. 35–94: Description of the Court of Love, enumeration of Love's barons. 95–324: Love addresses his ten barons, exhorting them in their work—Joy (109–24), Conversation (125–56), Boldness (157–80), Courtliness (181–94), Good Hope (195–216), Fear (217–48), Largesse (249–72), Love Service (273–84), Discretion (285–300) and Sweet Company (301–24). 325–44: Love asks Courtship to take prisoner anyone brought to her by his ten barons. 345–69: Ladies ask Love for his laws and he delegates Courtliness to make a judgement. 370–408: Courtliness says love is made of four things: good faith, loyalty, restraint and judgement. 409–16: The judgement is written down and called 'Earthly Paradise'.

416–708: The Courtliness of Love encases the judgement and then instructs how a lover can win over his lady (422–590) and how a lady should be groomed for the benefit of lovers and the dismay of jealous men (591–708). 709–25: Courtliness adds her own condemnation of jealousy. 726–80: Mercy arrives on horseback and complains to Love of Covetousness and Pride. 781–834: Love replies that through Mercy he will prevent ladies from being proud and that Courtliness has already dealt with them. 835–82: Coronation of Love.

883–902: Arrival of two jongleurs, Laughter and Distraction, and Lady Grace. 903–77: Laughter complains of slanderers. 978–1005: Pleasure replies that Courtliness has already condemned slanderers and that their influence positively increases the prudence of lovers. 1006–40: Distraction condemns inconstancy in lovers. 1041–67: Grace condemns hesitation in ladies. 1068–75: Arrival of Honour, Merit and the Bailiff of Love. 1076–83: Love tries to kiss Honour, but

is restrained. 1084–1126: Love asks Honour to grant him her love, and calls her his overlord. 1127–54: Honour acquiesces and condemns unseemly ladies. 1155–1253: The Bailiff of Love instructs maidens how to behave with their first love. 1254–1331: Merit instructs lovers how to behave with their lady. 1332–1560: Prowess condemns indolence and demonstrates how a messenger can persuade a lady. 1561–97: Love's jewellery cases are opened and the lovers dance in the sight of his barons. 1598–1615: Love Service proclaims Love's mastery.
  1616–22: The barons ask Love to stop the dance as some ladies are still merciless. 1623–46: Love has Pleasure stop the dance, then pledges to wage war on Pride. 1647–1717: Judgement pledges his support in the battle and condemns gossip and slander. 1718–21: Youth stands up. At this point the text breaks off.

A New Reading of the *Cort d'Amor*

The Court of Love is a feature of medieval texts which remains little studied. Early interest therein amongst medievalists from Raynouard and Diez onwards was centred on the question of whether courts in which aristocratic ladies gave judgements regarding particular problems in amorous matters actually existed or not. However, since this question has been shown to stem largely from misguided comments by Jean de Nostredame in the sixteenth century, interest in courts of love has waned.[42] Two textual traditions can nevertheless be distinguished: courts of love of the type just mentioned, judicial institutions with human ladies presiding, and the Court of Love, an allegorical court (in the wider sense) inhabited by personifications. Yet these two traditions are not totally separable either, for the Court of Love frequently serves as a site of judicial recourse, in texts such as the knight and cleric debates,[43] *Le Fablel dou Dieu d'Amors* and *De Vénus la Déesse d'Amor*.[44]

  The Court of Love in the *Cort d'Amor* certainly has a judicial function, producing a legal judgement (ll. 351–420), and being a site where complaints may be lodged against proud ladies and slanderers (for example, ll. 726–80, 903–77). It is also a court for lovers, a *locus amoenus* where those favoured by Love feast and dance and make merry, and it is their stronghold against courtly vices such as Orgueil and Vilania. What is unusual about the *Cort d'Amor* amongst Court of Love texts is that none of the chief protagonists is human. Humans are present at the court, and sometimes humans elsewhere send personifications, such as Merce, to plead at the court on their behalf, but no named individual human enters the court. Similarly, whilst in other texts the Court of Love is somewhere to be sought out, to be reached, the *Cort d'Amor* is unusual in that the court is the locus of the whole text.[45] In order to appreciate the significance of the centrality of the court and of the absence of individual humans, we need first to consider the role of the court within the text and the status of the text.

The *Cort d'Amor* designates itself as a *roman* four times in the opening sixteen lines (ll. 5, 10, 13, 16), a remarkable insistence, especially for a work which does not immediately show the characteristics we usually associate with a medieval romance. Of course, medieval generic terms are notoriously vague, and *roman*, at least originally, meant little more than a work written in a vernacular Romance language as opposed to Latin. Octosyllabic rhyming couplets are hardly unique to works designated as *romans*,[46] so the appellation is not merely formal. However, we can say that the term *roman* is generally associated with narrative structures,[47] and from Chrétien de Troyes onwards was classed separately from history, hagiography and the *fabliau* at least.[48] This definition of exclusion does not give us a very clear idea of what was intended by the insistent generic designations at the start of our text, but the narrative association is more revealing. Although all previous scholarship has denied the existence of a narrative framework in this text, it is nonetheless, as I shall demonstrate below, an allegorical narrative. I think that the repetition of the term *roman* is a signal that this is a narrative, and forewarns the audience that it is to be understood as such. If our text is indeed older than Guillaume de Lorris's *Roman de la Rose*, Guillaume can no longer be accorded the honour of having invented the allegorical romance, although admittedly his work differs greatly from the *Cort d'Amor* in both scope and ambition.

The opening of the *Cort d'Amor* suggests that it was designed for oral performance (*auzatz*, l. 5) within a courtly setting (given the elevated, courtly style of the verse). Right from the outset it proclaims a didactic purpose:

> Que lo be que lo romanz di
> fasson las dompnas e·l drut fi
> e gardon se de la folia,
> que·l romanz deveda e castia.

15

This is the first time in the text that women are mentioned, and it is made clear that the instruction concerns them as well as men. The addressees at the very start of the text, however, were male ([S]*einor*, l. 1). There is then an obscure reference to some previous occasion or text:

> Per so han fag novella amor
> d'una domna de gran valor
> viij.xx. que donas qe pulsellas,
> q'an trobat lurs raszons novellas
> coment amors sia lials.   25

Who is the *domna de gran valor*? Who are the *donas qe pulsellas*? And on what occasion did they judge on the legality/loyalty of love? Unfortunately it is difficult to say with any certainty, but what is certain is that the reference is to a previous occasion at which ladies engaged in judicial debate on amatory matters. Debate on issues of love, sometimes involving women, is to be found in certain lyric genres of the late twelfth and thirteenth centuries: the *tenso*, the *partimen* and the *joc partit*, but the reference in our text does not seem to be to a single debate such as would be represented by a lyric poem.

The second book of Andreas Capellanus' *De amore*, however, contains twenty-one judgements on love, attributed to aristocratic ladies in the 1170s.[49] In each case, the basic pattern is that Andreas presents a problem, such as whether greater love exists between lovers or a married couple (9), followed by the judgement of an aristocratic lady (Ermengarde de Narbonne in this case). In one case (16), Countess Marie de Champagne summons sixty ladies to help her adjudicate, in another (18) a court of ladies is assembled in Gascony at the behest of the army of Love. We have no evidence that these references are to actual historical courts,[50] but that is of relatively little importance in that they give us a clue as to what is being referred to in the *Cort d'Amor*. Andreas' text, more clearly than any other medieval testimony, indicates that there was a literary and possibly also a court tradition of women discussing and arbitrating in matters of love. Nothing relates *De amore* to the *Cort d'Amor* conclusively, but a number of elements suggest that Andreas' text may be being referred to in ll. 21–5 of our poem. Firstly, the number of women involved—although the *De amore* does not have precisely 160 ladies involved in any of the judgements, eight score (like sixty in *De amore* judgement 16) is probably simply chosen to indicate a large number. Secondly, the particular ladies mentioned—Andreas cites Marie de Champagne,

Eleanor d'Aquitaine, Ermengarde de Narbonne and Isobel de Vermandois, all of whom had associations with the troubadours. Thirdly, further textual similarities between the two works—they are both arts of love, both involve frequent dialogue, both cite the authority of a certain Johannitius (on which see the note to l. 108, below), and both feature an allegorical representation of the Court of Love.[51] If we cannot go so far as to assume a direct intertextual reference to *De amore*, we can at least say that the *Cort d'Amor* refers to something very like it. The gallicisms in our text suggest circulation in northern courts such as that of Marie de Champagne, and what we know about the early transmission of the *Cort d'Amor* does not rule out a date of composition contemporaneous with the *De Amore*.[52]

What of the *domna de gran valor* and the *novella amor*? The *domna* could be a contemporary lady such as Marie de Champagne, but in that case, why would she not be referred to by name? I think that what is being expressed in ll. 21-2 is that the eight score ladies have created a new, feminine, type of love, either for a lady (i.e. any lady) of great worth, or out of a lady of great worth (i.e., have personified love as a noblewoman). The *Cort d'Amor* sets itself up as a reply to this previous female view of love, which is why the opening addressees are specifically male and also why the gender of the personifications is crucial to understanding the text. Given that what little criticism has been devoted to this text has taken quite opposing views on the gender of Amor in particular, this is an issue which needs to be established early on.

In gender-marked languages, noun gender usually determines the sex of any personification. One frequent exception to this is Amor, owing to his/her literary pedigree. The god descended from antiquity only features to any significant extent in Apuleius' *Metamorphoses*, where he displays little power, relying on Jupiter's help to obtain the object of his desire, Psyche. Nor is Amor/Cupid the only deity associated primarily with love, the goddess Venus featuring more prominently in late antique texts such as the epithalamia of Sidonius and Claudian. Medieval goddesses of love also owe much to the assimilation of Fortuna—a fickle goddess spinning the wheel of fate to the dismay of powerless lovers. Added to these traditions the fact that the noun *amor* is masculine in Latin and in Old French (*amour*) but feminine in Occitan, there is no *a priori* reason to attribute either gender to Amor in our text.

Of the critics who consider Amor to be a woman, the only one who seeks to justify the claim systematically is Jones, but her argument is linguistically inept:

> The author of the *Cort d'Amor* had considerable difficulty remembering (or believing) that his heroine was in fact a woman. Ordinarily *Fin'Amor* is designated in the text by feminine pronouns (e.g. l. 351 *leis*), but she is designated at least ten times by masculine words as if she were a man [...]. In one passage *Fin'Amor* is compared to a man.[53]

Jones's one example is erroneous, as *leis* (l. 351) is a noun, not a pronoun. Furthermore, with only one exception, there are no feminine forms applied to Amor anywhere in the text. He is *lo* (ll. 48, 353, 1080), *el* (ll. 354, 872, 879, 899, 1078, 1592) and *celui* (l. 1092); he is *umils* (l. 765) and *gentils* (l. 766); he is a *seinor* (ll. 838, 871, 979, 992, 1125, 1575, 1686) and a *rei* (ll. 839, 903); he courts Honor in the role of a male lover, calling himself her *sers* (l. 1101) and her *hom* (l. 1109), and he is likened to a *seinor* (ll. 97, 103, 124, 353, 779), a *sabis hom* (l. 100) and an *om pros* (l. 123). This list of gender-marked references to Amor is exhaustive except for the very first reference to him where he is coupled with feminine adjectives:

> Ora zuzatz coment araszona
> sa gent Amors la dousa e la bona.   30

Thus whilst we can unreservedly state that Amor is presented as a male personification in the *Cort d'Amor*, we need to explain why 'he' is undeniably a 'she' at l. 30. The explanation is related to the obscure reference in ll. 21–5 and the masculine addressees of l. 1. The introduction (ll. 1–34) as a whole announces that this is a text addressed to men, produced in response to a prior, female, vision of love. Line 30 is simply heavy irony; the introduction could be paraphrased as: 'you have heard what a court of women has said about Love, well now listen to what "*She*" has to say on the subject . . .'. Finally, for the sake of thoroughness, we should record that *amor*, when not personified, remains feminine. This is evident in ll. 21, 264, 322, 977, 987, 1059, 1093, 1371, 1543 and 1548. In each of these cases the reference is clearly either to the concept of love in general or to a particular love between two people, not to a personification.

The introduction, therefore, prepares us for a Court of Love governed by a reactionary male personification in which 'female' views on love are challenged. In the exhortation of both men and women to follow the instruction propounded (ll. 13–16), the universality of the art of love is proclaimed, but this in no way prevents the governing discourse being announced as a resolutely male one. Realizing this is essential to comprehending the text. Only once we appreciate the gender issue can we understand either the structure and purpose of the debate or the nature of the allegorical narrative.

As an art of love (which, despite its announced didacticism, it does not generically claim to be), the *Cort d'Amor* is somewhat unusual. Certainly it does not fit into the impressively fixed Occitan genre of the *ensenhamen*, simply because its instruction is not univocal.[54] It does share some common ground with the *ensenhamens* in terms of individual points of advice, but the difference in approach is highlighted by a proposition in the earliest *ensenhamen*, Garin lo Brun's *Ensenhamen alla domna* (incipit, *E·l tremini d'estiu*):

> Savis hom ama apen[d]re
> e·l fols ama contendre.[55]   174

> [The wise man likes to learn
> and the foolish man likes to argue.]

In opposing differing discourses on love, the *Cort d'Amor* shows an affinity with Ovid's *Ars amatoria* and Andreas Capellanus' *De amore*, even if the Occitan text is much more compact and maintains a courtly rather than a learned register. Indeed, individual points of detail demonstrate that the author of our text was familiar with these more illustrious and verbose arts of love.[56] Whilst Ovid and Andreas sometimes use allegory to ornament their didactic discourse, however, the author of the *Cort d'Amor* presents us with an allegory which contains didactic discourses. The work which undoubtedly most warrants comparison with our text is thus the *Roman de la Rose*, but whereas the more illustrious Old French work only deals with how to win a lady (corresponding to the first books of Ovid's and Andreas Capellanus' works), the *Cort d'Amor* also tackles the problems involved in *maintaining* a love relationship (corresponding to the second books of Ovid and Andreas).

The *Cort d'Amor* does not just have differing voices on the subject of love, but presents a dialogue between two opposing philosophies of love: on the one hand, a 'courtly' love in which sincerity, worth and the idolization of the beloved are fundamental; on the other hand, an 'Ovidian' love in which ruse, deceit and even force are advocated in the lover's pursuit of gratification.[57] The courtly version is the first expressed, in Amor's speeches to his ten barons and in the judgement made by Corteszia. Jung noticed that Amor's speeches constitute, together, a definition of courtly love,[58] but he did not remark that they are also sequential steps, *gradus amoris*. The hierarchy of Amor's barons is already expressed in their description (ll. 42–50):

> Zoi e Solasz foron lai sus
> e Ardimens e Corteszia
> qe de flors l'enzonchon la via.
> Bon'Esperancha e Paors   45
> li portent de denant las flors.
> D'autra part Larguesza e Domneis
> lo meton en un leit d'orfreis.
> Celars e Dousa Conpania
> geton desus ruesa floria.   50

Joi and Solaz, apart from being on top of Parnassus with Amor, are the only two barons to merit the noble title *Don* (ll. 109, 137) and represent, respectively, the culmination and the start of courtship. The other barons are then presented in ascending and, in Amor's speeches, sequential order, which amongst other things explains why both fear and boldness are praised.[59] A lover must obviously be bold enough to aspire to love in the first place, but once he has told his lady of that love it is fitting that he should not be too sure of himself. That the sequence together constitutes courtship is then expressed by Amor addressing Drudaria, telling her to receive any lovers brought to her by the other ten barons.

Although Amor specifically addresses his barons (l. 40), and specifically addresses them as men (*seniors*, l. 101), it is ladies at the court who promise to obey him (ll. 347–50) and who ask him for the laws of love (ll. 351–62). Amor chooses Corteszia to make this judgement on courtly love for him. Corteszia judges what laws ought to be respected in love, so it is not a judgement in the sense of choosing between two positions. Indeed, the judgement actually provokes rather than resolves debate, for Cortesa d'Amor, immediately after encasing the judgement, says:

> 'Aves auszit lo zutgament
> qan adreitaments an zutgat,
> mas, qar sai qe m'en sabreitz grat,
> vos dirai d'amor de tal loc,   425
> don maint plor tornaran en ioc
> e maint joc tornaran en plor.
> Q'aital usatge han amador ...

The *mas* in l. 424 expresses exception to the judgement, *ioc* indicates a ludic attitude, and the chiasmus of ll. 426–7 a duality at odds with the ideology of the courtly vision. The mention of *amador* in line 428 is in contrast with the ladies who had listened to Amor's speeches to his barons and asked for laws to follow, and thus the Cortesa d'Amor's following instruction on the functioning of love is not merely Ovidian but associated with men (even if she does also go on to give advice on a lady's grooming). She gives another sequential account of courtship,[60] but from a capricious, cynical point of view. For example, whereas Amor praised Paor for making the sincerity and emotional engagement of a lover manifest (ll. 217–24), Cortesa d'Amor tells a lover to 'pretend' to die (l. 468) and to cry 'so that' he can 'steal' the heart of his lady (ll. 473–4).

The courtly/Ovidian dialectic is thus associated with the female/male distinction announced at the start. Unless these two axes are understood, the dynamic of the whole work is lost, and yet Jones's edition even manages to efface the distinction between Corteszia and Cortesa d'Amor, reading them as one character. (To counter the problem of Corteszia thus replying to herself at l. 709, she proposes the insertion of another female speaker at l. 657, and she comments on passages such as the advocating of gifts to win favours as having 'a distinctly Ovidian flavor that is quite separate from the general tone of the rest of the poem'.)[61] In fact, their speeches allow us not only to distinguish but also to define them. Corteszia is courtliness in an absolute sense, representing a whole ethos of courtly behaviour. Cortesa d'Amor is the use of courtly codes to achieve aims in love. One reason why this dialectic has not proved more obvious is Amor's ambivalent position in relation to the two sides, censuring neither. Both coexist peacefully at his court, two types of courtliness relating to two species of love united by a common genus.

Whilst Jung notices (indeed was the first to notice) the courtly/Ovidian tension between Corteszia and Cortesa d'Amor, he does not see it as being maintained throughout the work, considering rather that the 'amour courtois' of Amor and Corteszia at the start is succeeded by a variety of individual perspectives from personifications later in the work.[62] Certainly the dialogue is not always to the fore, and this is because of the common ground between the two sides. Thus when Corteszia responds to Cortesa d'Amor's cynical speech, she begins *d'aiso m'acort eu ben ab vos* (on this point I agree with you, l. 710), because she shares her interlocutor's disdain for jealous men.

Therefore the attacks on slanderers from Ris and Deport (ll. 903–77, 1006–40) are not strictly speaking either courtly or Ovidian, the *lausengiers* constituting a common enemy to all lovers. That said, Plaser does reply to Ris that fear of slanderers can improve the courtly lover, a proposition that marks him as a restrained courtly form of pleasure contrasting with the Ovidian exuberance of Ris and Deport. More clearly defined is the opposition between Honor, Baillessa d'Amor and Valor, on one side, and Proessa, on the other. The former three condemn dissimulation, and instruct courtly maidens and lovers in the maintenance of a sincere relationship, but Proessa clearly expresses his exception to their discourses:

> ... 'Eu no·m soi entremessa   1335
> ad aqesta cort(z) de parlar;
> ez hai auzit a totz comtar,
> per Crist, bonas raszos e bellas;
> mais eu vos comtarai novellas,
> qe no·s taignon ges entre vos,   1340
> qe fan li fol drut nuailos.

He starts by condemning indolence in lovers, something the three personifications who spoke before him had been concerned with too, but Proessa goes on to say that with a little effort a lover can win himself not just one, but a number of ladies (ll. 1377–80), and continues with an account of how to use a rhetorically accomplished messenger to good advantage. Once again, the disagreement provokes not animosity but celebration, with a dance starting again. In what remains of the work an attack is made on another common enemy, Orgueil, by Sens and Amor, and nothing is preserved of Joven's speech, the text breaking off just as he takes the floor, so we have no clear evidence as to a resolution of the courtly/Ovidian dialectic, even if the gendered thematics announced in the introduction leads us to expect the triumph of the latter.

Having examined the dialogic nature of the instruction, and the gendered status of the text, I now turn to the question of allegory. The fact that the *Cort d'Amor* is incomplete in its one manuscript attestation has not facilitated its allegorical reading, and a general failure to read the text allegorically has no doubt led to an underestimation of its quality. The absence of individual humans makes a 'psychological' reading difficult, and the absence of personified vices from the court threatens to render a 'universalizing' reading colourless although, as Jung notices, Sens's offer to take arms with Amor against Orgueil at the end of our fragment may well indicate an ensuing psychomachia in the lost section of the work. In any case, the relative sparseness of narrative as compared with the direct speeches is a distraction from any allegorical reading, and the start of the text provides few clues as to what the narrative might signify. In this, the *Cort d'Amor* is unlike the *Roman de la Rose*, which despite similarly favouring direct discourse clearly signals both its narrative course and its allegorical meaning (or at least a promise thereof) from the very start.

As even the literal text has been little understood, as the foregoing account of the love debate in the work has shown, it is no wonder that any allegorical subtext should have remained undiscovered. Where the narrative is skeletal or absent, the speeches made are our best or only guide to the personifications. Jung, however, maintains that the speeches are not always closely identifiable with the notions personified, and Taylor calls the speeches in the latter part of the work unconnected.[63] This does not stand up to examination, however. I shall shortly come back to the chief personification, Amor, but first let us consider the other personifications.

Amor's ten barons are Joi, Solaz, Corteszia, Ardimen, Bon' Esperansa, Paor, Larguesza, Dompneis, Celamen and Dousa Compaina, who, as I have established, constitute a sequential account of courtship. Apart from Joi, Corteszia and Dompneis, none of them plays any further part in the work, and only Corteszia and Dompneis later get to speak. Drudaria and Pretz are the keys (l. 76) or guardians (ll. 325–44) of love. Cortesa d'Amor is, as seen above, a particular use of courtliness in love. Merce comes to the court to complain of merciless ladies. Ris, Deport and Plaser discuss the ways in which slanderers suppress laughter, distraction and pleasure. Coindia tells how a lady should be graceful with a worthy lover. Honor elaborates how a lady can achieve honour. Baillessa d'Amor explains how a maiden should keep her lover. Valor describes how a lover must be worthy to keep his lady. Proessa tells of the prowess of a dynamic lover. Sens condemns folly. We do not know what Joven is about to say when the text breaks off, but if he were not to speak about youth and its merits or troubles, he would be the only personification, *pace* Jung, not to speak of the notion he personifies. What throws Jung and Taylor off the track is no doubt the fact that the personifications are not obsessively concerned with their names or introspective in their discourse. Honor, for example, says that a lady should not hesitate too long in granting her lover what he desires, should not wear too much make-up, and should mind that she speaks nobly. The mere attribution of such contentions to her gives us a clear idea of what 'honour' is considered to consist in, even if she does not spell it out as such (and indeed hints at semantic shading with Valor by referring to ladies aspiring to merit (l. 1154)).

I have already demonstrated how the love debate structures the whole work, but there is also a narrative structure, and in order to elucidate it we need to read everything in relation to Amor. All of the personifications speak not only of their own concept but of their own concept in relation to love. Proessa, for instance, is prowess in love, not prowess in arms or in anything else, because here he falls under the lordship of Love and therefore the semantic extension of love. The allegorical narrative only becomes clear once we read Amor as a lover himself. His speeches to his ten barons show him engaged in courtship. The contrasting account of Cortesa d'Amor illustrates an alternative procedure. This is followed by the arrival of Merce, indicating, eventually, the consent of Amor's lady, and Amor's coronation by Joi, indicating Amor's success. The coronation provokes a number of events which metaphorically suggest physical consummation: the activation of the fountain (l. 843), an abundance of flowers (ll. 849–52) and the blazing of the Fire of Love (l. 855); this is confirmed by the watchman:

> 'Cobezesa es morta e aunida,
> e havem Orguel abatut.
> Ara si guardon li cornut,   870
> qe mon[s] senior[s] porta corona.'

Cobezesa and Orgueil, of whom Merce complained, have been defeated, and the jealous men of whom Corteszia and Cortesa d'Amor spoke are now cuckolds.

Once the relationship of Amor with an as yet unspecified lady has been consummated, the most important issue becomes secrecy. Discretion was, of course, important during the courtship, Celamen being one of Amor's ten barons and indeed distinguished from the other nine by being presented with Amor's banner (l. 300—a nice joke, giving Discretion a banner!), but now, there being something substantial to gossip about, the matter takes centre stage. Ris and Deport are jongleurs, representing the impulse to express the joy of love, and their complaint is against slanderers. Meanwhile the aristocratic Na Coindia, sister of Amor, advocates sustaining the effort of courtship once a lady has been agreeable to her lover. This theme is to be taken up by Honor, Baillessa d'Amor and Valor, but the arrival of Honor in particular provokes a most remarkable episode. Baillessa d'Amor places her next to Amor, who is so overcome with joy that he tries to kiss her there and then and has to be restrained by his attendants. This is one of the clearest indications that Amor is not as firmly in the courtly camp as his earlier behaviour may have made us believe. His misbehaviour is redolent of the classical gods, which may explain the situation of his court on Mount Parnassus (l. 41), but instead of the arrogance of a Jupiter, he demonstrates the submission of a courtly lover in addressing Honor—calling her his overlord (ll. 1125–6).

In the advice on the maintenance of a love relationship, two alternatives are again posited, as we have seen above, one by Honor, Baillessa d'Amor and Valor, the other by Proessa. As with Corteszia/Cortesa d'Amor on courtship, it is not evident which of the two Amor favours. His attraction towards Honor would suggest his predilection for the former camp, but the very impropriety of his advances towards her associate him with Proessa. It is also perhaps telling that on both occasions the orgiastic celebrations immediately follow the Ovidian alternative. Are we to understand that Amor tries both approaches, finding the cynical one more effective? In any case, his fortune seems to improve again here as he ordains festivities involving the opening of his jewellery cases, dancing and singing, and a public proclamation of his dominion from Dompneis, but this is interrupted by Amor's barons who complain that some women still do not dare to receive their lovers (ll. 1616–22). This provokes Amor once more to condemn Orgueil (who has evidently revived since his defeat proclaimed after the coronation), and Sens to speak out against boastfulness. The problem, as after the coronation, is one of discretion and the maintenance of a relationship.

Without the end to the work, it is unclear how, or if, the allegorical narrative is resolved. Jean de Meun ensured that Guillaume de Lorris's rose did get plucked in the end, but in the *Cort d'Amor* the consummation of love as represented by the coronation of Amor occurs after fewer than 900 lines, at roughly the mid point of what remains of the work, and the opening of Amor's coffers may well indicate a second conquest. I suspect that the ending would have further endorsed the Ovidian approach to love, perhaps even by means of an event so obviously scurrilous that the truncation of the ending may be attributable to censorship. There is certainly evidence of censorship in the lacunae in the rest of the text. Of the twelve instances where there definitely seem to be lines omitted, six (following ll. 1038, 1086, 1185, 1348, 1418, 1654) are in explicitly physical contexts.

Rather than speculate further on the lost ending of the *Cort d'Amor*, I shall return to the allegory. I have given an outline of how the text can yield a coherent narrative because previous critics have failed to notice it, but, as with much secular allegorical narrative, a much more interesting reading is produced by examining how that narrative deconstructs itself. No sooner is a courtly course of behaviour advocated than an Ovidian alternative is provided, and it is not clear which Amor follows. Conflicting discourses are juxtaposed with little or no comment on their relative value. Distinctions between allegory and literality are also blurred by the skeletal nature of the personification and the predominance of human discourse.

Although the only named characters are the personifications, there are certainly humans present at the court. The personifications, as we have seen, frequently address these humans, and Amor instructs Drudaria to either chastise or welcome humans brought to the court by his ten barons, according to whether they are engaged in a relationship or not. The one human individual present, even if he remains nameless, is the *gaita*, the watchman (ll. 77, 867). This figure, borrowed from the *alba*, is an indication that the Court of Love is, amongst other things, a metaphor for the physical union of lovers, and it is he who heralds the consummation of Amor's relationship.

The principal rhetorical device of the personifications, and of the work, is the voicing of exemplary lovers. This form of *amplificatio* is one of the standard rhetorical structures in the Middle Ages,[64] and it is used to a remarkable extent in the *Cort d'Amor*. Some personifications (Ris, Valor, Proessa) do little other than voice speeches or dialogues of sample lovers, and on several occasions the encasement is doubled, with the lovers themselves engaging in internal dialogues (ll. 229–46), apostrophizing some of their own faculties (ll. 801–3) or God (ll. 1187–92), and voicing further exemplars such as robbers (ll. 1198–9), servants (ll. 1295–7) or public opinion (ll. 1309–11). In Proessa's speech, the messenger, whilst addressing his lord's lady, voices not only his lord's sentiments (ll.

1444–62), but also what the lady to whom he is speaking might say (ll. 1500–1). All of these sample speeches and dialogues are not just a gloss on the narrative, as the instruction of Amor in the *Roman de la Rose* can be read as a gloss on the allegorical narrative;[65] rather, they actually provide the narrative flesh on the meagre bones of the allegorical narrative. Yet this part of the narrative could itself be described as allegorical in that it is presented as hypothetical discourse. That this narrative has never before been spotted by a critic is due to the fact that the couple involved are never individuated beyond being 'a lover' and 'a lady' and it is therefore not clear (nor is it necessary) that the same lover and lady might be involved on each occasion. Thus whilst the individuality of the 'personification' Amor is promoted, so is the exemplary, universal nature of the 'individual' sample lover and his lady.

The *Cort d'Amor* is subversive in its use of personification, and can thus be shown to engage in one of the most celebrated philosophical debates of the twelfth and thirteenth centuries: the universals debate.[66] Whilst personification might immediately seem to favour a realist philosophy—portraying universals as things—this text demonstrates the nominalist tenet that universals are just ways of talking about similar individuals, and it does so by blurring the distinction between universal personification and unnamed individual. What is the difference between Love and a lover, or rather, how can one exist distinct from the other? Not at all, it would seem, on the basis of this text. Although the courtly trappings and occasional proclamation of his power (e.g. l. 872) present Amor as a powerful cosmic force, that image is constantly undermined by his foolish behaviour, by the failure of his judgement to still argument, and by the constantly renewed complaints against Orgueil and slanderers. In Proessa's speech, where he starts to voice what a messenger should say to convince a lady of his lord's worth, we find this passage:

>   Ja no·m sal Christus
>   s'ieu non sai, bella dompna e bona,   1405
>   qi porta de Ioi la corona
>   sobre lo(u)s amadors del mon.
>   E vos baizares m'en lo fron
>   senpres qant eu lo vos dirai.
>   Qe lo joventz q'en vos estai   1410
>   e·l vergoigna qi ren non tria
>   vos en fara faire folia.

> q'el n'es be de xx. parts semos.
> Mais eu lo lauzava a vos
> e dic vos qe sots lo solel   1415
> non haura bazaler parel.

The reference in line 1/406 to the bearer of the crown of Joi indicates that he is speaking of Amor, yet ll. 1414–16 and what follows indicate that he is speaking of his lord, the lover that he is recommending. The distinction between Amor and a lover is again demolished, as when Amor lunged at Honor, but here it is done in a human context. Although this ambiguity is particularly foregrounded and explored in the narrative context of the *Cort d'Amor*, it is commonly found in troubadour lyrics. *Amor* can refer to a deity, to the notion of love, or to the beloved her-/himself. Instances of this are too numerous to cite, but the songs of Jaufre Rudel, Bernart de Ventadorn and Peire Vidal, to name but three, are replete with examples.

The blurring of individual and universal is not restricted to the portrayal of Amor. Amor addresses both Larguesza and Celamen as lovers embodying the qualities they represent, and Proessa adopts the role of a lover (ll. 1375–6). In the case of Larguesza and Proessa, this portrayal involves syllepsis, as it did with Amor: Larguesza and Proessa both being qualities associated with men in this text, their grammatical gender is overridden.[67] The case is more ambivalent with (grammatically feminine) Merce. Despite being *vista* (l. 729), he is *aqest* (l. 733), *le vasals* (l. 736) and *el* (l. 739). It is also striking that Merce comes to Amor to complain that ladies are not being merciful. We would expect the gift of mercy to be within Merce's power, and his portrayal as a man therefore seems to suggest that no man can govern something so firmly in the female domain. That four of the thirty personifications in the text are sylleptically portrayed constitutes a significant stylistic feature, given that of the scores of personifications in the *Roman de la Rose* only one (or two, depending on the manuscripts used) abandon their grammatical gender.[68] Furthermore, seven personifications—Ardimen, Bon'Esperansa, Dompneis, Dousa Compaina, Drudaria, Vilania and Fals'Amor—have no gender-marked traits at all, beyond their grammatical gender as substantives. Thus not only does this text undermine a realist attitude towards personification, it also questions the gendering of abstractions.

If the *Cort d'Amor*'s play on universals and individuals undermines established medieval exegetical techniques, the same is true of metaphor in the text. The two ubiquitous elements are flowers and birds, which permeate the lyric tradition as metaphors for ladies and lovers, respectively. Flowers and birds constitute a further set of signifiers at the court, coexisting with the personifications and the humans:

> Qant venc al intrar del castel,
> comenson a cantar li aucel,
> e·l Foc d'Amor ad abrasar, 855
> e las donzellas a dansar;
> e l'amador canton dous lais.
> Tan rica cort no er'iamais!
> Pels deis si asezon matenent,
> las flors els ausels mesclament; 860
> el mon no es volta ni lais
> l'ausel non canto en palais.

We are told that a lady is, amongst base people, a rose between nettles (ll. 958–61), and a rose in the garden of Amor (ll. 1260–1); there is also an abundance of flowers throughout the work: Amor's barons strew and carry flowers to and for Amor (ll. 43–50), a lily crowns the fountain (l. 93), violets and lilies throw themselves into Amor's sight and all other flowers honour him at his coronation (ll. 849–52) and so on. Yet flowers are not just metaphors for ladies. Another common metaphor is the flower as potential: something which has not yet become fruit. Thus Celamen is the flower of the joy of love (ll. 285–6), the *lausengiers* destroy flowers to prevent love being fruitful (ll. 924–30) and judgement can help the joy of love blossom and bear fruit (ll. 1252–3). In other cases, it is not clear what flowers are supposed to signify, such as Amor's coffers full of flowers, the strewing of those flowers on the floor (ll. 1581–4) and lovers throwing their ladies a flower each (l. 1597). Finally, Amor gives Merce a flower to give to lovers 'as a sign' (*per entresenia*, l. 819) that they should have all that they want. Flowers are the ultimate sliding signifier in this text, and the opening [S]*einor, vos que volez la flor / e la cortesia d'amor* (ll. 1–2) is majestically vague.

Their common singing endeavour no doubt stands at the origin of birds being metaphors for lovers (e.g. ll. 853–62, quoted above), but this association is not consistently maintained in the speeches. When Amor tells Solaz how a bird flees from a trap he has spotted, the bird is associated with a *vilan*, keeping his wife from an *ome cortes* (ll. 133–40). Cortesa d'Amor says that a lady must mind her appearance as a nobleman grooms a sparrow hawk (ll. 591–7) and that a nightingale would sooner be tamed than a noble lady induced to say anything unseemly (ll. 640–2). Baillessa d'Amor associates the lover with a bird, but in the context of a lady as a bird-catcher luring and then destroying him (compare Amor's speech to Ardimen, where the young girl is afraid of a chirping bird, ll. 159–60), and this image is refined by Proessa, who says that a lady kills the courtly lover like a nightingale who dies because once taken captive he cannot be with his partner. Finally, in Sens' speech, slanderers kill lovers (and their ladies) like an archer who shoots a bird. The bird can thus be a lover, a lady or an unworthy man, and the bird-catcher can be a lady or a slanderer. Like flowers, birds recur in metaphors and similes to demonstrate the instability of signs.

It is probably because the *Cort d'Amor* is so subversive as an allegory that it has not been recognized as one. Modern dislike of allegory tends to stem from a view of allegory as a process whereby the nutshell of the allegory is utterly discarded once the fruit of the 'meaning' has been discovered, although the few popular allegories, such as the *Roman de la Rose*, are notorious for frustrating such simple hermeneutic impulses. In our text, it is impossible to separate what is allegorical from what is literal, and although clear dichotomies are established between courtly and Ovidian love and between female and male views of love, they are then studiously undermined. The same is true of any sense of hierarchy in the court. Amor is proclaimed second only to Christ (ll. 838–40), and addresses God as his overlord (ll. 879–80), but he defers to Corteszia to make his judgement for him, wears the crown of Joi, is unable to dispel the threat of Orgueil permanently, and describes Honor as his overlord (ll. 1125–6). Even more surprisingly, he also invokes himself whilst donning the mantle of a lover to woo Honor (ll. 1109–12). It is no doubt this passage that led Hentsch to see Fin'Amor as a separate character, but Fin'Amor is simply used as a synonym for Amor elsewhere in the text (ll. 58, 734, 885, 1588). Again, a realist hierarchy concertinas to demonstrate the universal as nothing more than a way of speaking about the individual.

Whilst I have thus far been stressing the intellectual ambition of the *Cort d'Amor*, it is not just an empty if brilliant verbal display. Medieval poetics is frequently obsessed with forms of expression, but that is part and parcel of any attempt to voice thought and emotion. The author of our text was certainly no hack, piecing together tired topoi and standard didactic fare: even Lafont and Anatole grudgingly describe the language as elegant (see above). Instead, the author blends elements of different genres in an original and entertaining way. Certainly there is a good deal of didactic material, but it is always starkly juxtaposed with alternative advice. There is also frequent humour, as we have seen, whilst the speeches put into the mouths of sample lovers sometimes reach considerable heights of poetic grace and emotional feeling. For instance, Baillessa d'Amor voices the sentiments of a *doncella* who has slept with her companion and who tenderly proclaims her love whilst expressing the fear of betrayal (ll. 1166–1221).[69] Valor, by way of reply, then presents the case of the lover reassuring his lady with proclamations of service and throwing himself unconditionally at her mercy (ll. 1275–1331). These speeches work by way of contrast with the Ovidian material precisely by contriving to strike us with their sincerity, even if the text as a whole works to undermine such hermeneutic transparency. Even in the use of standard medieval tropes, the author demonstrates originality and subtlety. Instead of the usual tautology whereby personifications are allowed to illustrate their own concept and nothing else, we are presented with a complex semantic web which explores, for instance, the relationship between laughter and discretion, or between merit and honour.

The *Cort d'Amor* is an eloquent celebration of the many manifestations of love which has languished on the sidelines of medieval studies for too long. It has much of interest for a multitude of genres and critical approaches, including the interface of lyric and narrative, gendered discourse, the history of allegorical romance, and allegorical tropes more generally. Whilst it has not been possible to do more than touch on some of these facets in this introduction, I hope that the long-overdue production of a reasonably reliable and available critical edition and translation will provide a stimulus for interest in the work. In order to enact (and appreciate) the effect of the *Cort d'Amor*, we are told that it is necessary to be courtly (ll. 9–12). The work is targeted at those who desire the flower and the courtliness of love (ll. 1–2). Given the implications of these terms of exclusion, I would think twice before calling it either 'insipide' or 'décousu'.

Notes to the Introduction

1. François Zufferey, *Recherches linguistiques sur les chansonniers provençaux*, Publications romanes et françaises 176 (Geneva: Droz, 1987), 104, notes that 'le copiste de *L* avait aussi l'intention de retenir un passage du roman allégorique de *La Cour d'Amour*, dont le début nous est conservé par *N* (fol. 31–46): au bas du fol. 111[v], en effet, apparaissent les mots de réclame *Seignor vos que volez la flor*,

mais ils ont été biffés à la suite d'une modification dans l'agencement du manuscrit'. Zufferey points out that L and N are both Italian chansonniers. For a full list of the contents of N, see Curt Ferdinand Bühler, 'The Phillipps Manuscript of Provençal Poetry now MS. 819 of the Pierpont Morgan Library', *Speculum* 22 (1947), 68–74.
2. See Hermann Suchier, 'Il canzoniere provenzale di Cheltenham', *Rivista di filologia romanza* 2 (1875), 49–52, 144–72; and Joseph Anglade, 'Pour l'histoire du chansonnier provençal N', *Romania* 53 (1927), 225.
3. See J. J. and M. J. De Bure, *Catalogue des livres rares et précieux de la bibliothèque de feu M. le comte de Mac-Carthy Reagh* (Paris: Crapelet, 1815), no. 2809; *Catalogus librorum manuscriptorum in bibliotheca D. Thomae Phillips* (Middlehill: [n.pub.], 1837), no. 8335; Alfred Jeanroy, *Bibliographie sommaire des chansonniers provençaux* (Paris: Champion, 1916), 10; Alfred Pillet and Henry Carstens, *Bibliographie der Troubadours*, Schriften der Königsberger Gelehrten Gesellschaft: Sonderreihe 3 (Halle: Niemeyer, 1933; repr. New York: Franklin, 1968), p. xviii; Clovis Félix Brunel, *Bibliographie des manuscrits littéraires en Ancien Provençal*, Société de Publications romanes et françaises 13 (Paris, 1935; repr. Geneva: Slatkine; Marseille: Lafitte, 1973), 4. All of these date N as 14th- or 15th-cent. without seeking to justify the claim. Suchier, 'Il canzoniere', 49–52, dates the script as 14th-cent. Italian.
4. Giuseppe Frasso, 'Petrarca, Andrea da Mantova e il canzoniere provenzale N', *Italia medioevale e umanistico* 17 (1974), 185–205 (205).
5. Meta Harrsen and George K. Boyce, *Italian manuscripts in the Pierpont Morgan Library* (New York: Pierpont Morgan Library, 1953), 9.
6. Gianfranco Folena, 'Tradizione e cultura trobadorica nelle corti e nelle città venete', in *Storia della cultura veneta* (Vicenza: Neri Pozza, 1976), 453–562 (463). Folena acknowledges that at the time Harrsen and Boyce were writing, it was generally thought that Gaibana was an illustrator.
7. D'Arco Silvio Avalle, *I manoscritti della letteratura in lingua d'oc*, new edn. rev. L. Leonardi (Turin: Einaudi, 1993), 81. Avalle also remarks that 'le influenze bizantine ancora sensibili nell'Epistolario sono totalmente assenti in N, dove invece il tratto rivela una certa apertura verso i moduli gotici'.
8. Bernhard Degenhart and Annegrit Schmitt, *Corpus der Italienischen Zeichnungen*, II x 4 vols. (Berlin: Mann, 1980), II/i., 27 and 34.
9. François Avril et al. (eds)., *Manuscrits enluminés d'origine italienne*, 2 vols. (Paris: Bibliothèque nationale, 1984), ii. XIIIe siècle, ed. François Avril and M. T. Gousset, with C. Rabel, 1–2.
10. Roger Sherman Loomis and Laura Hibbard Loomis, *Arthurian Legends in Medieval Art*, Modern Languages of America Monograph Series, 1938 (repr. New York: Kraus, 1975), 116.
11. Lowanne E. Jones, *The 'Cort d'Amor': A Thirteenth-Century Allegorical Art of Love*, North Carolina Studies in the Romance Languages and Literatures 185 (Chapel Hill: University of North Carolina Press, 1977), 12.
12. Ernest Langlois, *Origines et sources du Roman de la Rose*, Bibliothèque des Ecoles françaises d'Athènes et de Rome (Paris: Thorin, 1890), 9–10. Langlois does not mention the *Cort d'Amor*, but examines the commonplaces of early allegorical literature akin to our text.
13. On Constans's edition, see below.

14. Ernest Langlois, *Les Manuscrits du 'Roman de la Rose': description et classement*, Travaux et mémoires de l'université de Lille: Nouvelle série: I Droit, Lettres, 7 (Lille: Tallandier; Paris: Champion, 1910).
15. Sylvia Huot, *The Romance of the Rose and its Medieval Readers: Interpretation, Reception, Manuscript Transmission* (Cambridge: Cambridge University Press, 1993), 5.
16. David Hult, *Self-fulfilling Prophecies: Readership and Authority in the First 'Roman de la Rose'* (Cambridge: Cambridge University Press, 1986), 23.
17. Suchier, 'Il canzoniere', 51.
18. Cf. Paul Meyer, 'Les troisièmes personnes du pluriel en provençal', *Romania* 9 (1883), 192–215.
19. Suchier, 'Il canzoniere', 51, contests Raynouard's view that the manuscript is the result of assembled quires, and in any case our text contains Italian features as well as gallicisms.
20. Emmanuèle Baumgartner, 'Le roman aux XIIe et XIIIe siècles dans la littérature occitane', in *Grundriss der romanischen Literaturen des Mittelalters*, ed. Hans Robert Jauss and Erich Köhler, 13 vols. (Heidelberg: Winter, 1968–72), IV/i., 627–44 (627): 'Si on se limite en effet aux textes dont l'origine provençale est indiscutable, la liste est vite dressée. Il nous reste quelques brefs récits de caractère romanesque; les *novas* [...] et surtout deux œuvres remarquables et parfaitement isolées, *Jaufre, Flamenca*.'
21. Karl Bartsch, *Provenzalisches Lesebuch* (Elberfeld: Friderichs, 1855), 34–8.
22. Ibid. 34 n. Jones strangely claims that she does not know whether Bartsch, Mahn or someone else copied the text from the manuscript, although she does notice that Bartsch had not spotted the lack of continuity between ll. 484 and 505.
23. C. A. F. Mahn, *Gedichte der Troubadours*, 6 vols. (Berlin: Duemmler, 1856), ii. 168–71.
24. Léopold Constans, 'La cour d'Amour', *Revue des langues romanes* 20 (1881), 121–79, 209–20, 261–76.
25. Camille Chabaneau, 'Corrections', *Revue des langues romanes* 21 (1882), 90–8; Emil Levy, 'Corrections', ibid. 238–9.
26. Léopold Constans, *Les Manuscrits provençaux de Cheltenham (Angleterre)* (Paris: Maisonneuve, 1882), 66–115. Henceforth all references to Constans, unless otherwise stated, will be to this edition.
27. René Lavaud and René Nelli, *Les Troubadours*, 2 vols. (Bruges: Desclée de Brouwer, 1960–6), ii. 236–43.
28. Linda Paterson, review of Lowanne E. Jones, *The 'Cort d'Amor'*, *French Studies* 35 (1981), 425.
29. Léopold Constans, 'Le songe vert', *Romania* 33 (1904), 490–539 (491).
30. William Allan Neilson, *The Origins and Sources of the Court of Love*, Studies and Notes in Philology and Literature 6 (Boston: Ginn, 1899), 30.
31. Albert Stimming, 'Provenzalische Literatur', in *Grundriss der romanischen Philologie*, ed. Gustav Gröber, 2 vols. (Strassburg: Trübner, 1888–1902), ii. 45.
32. Alice Adèle Hentsch, *De la littérature didactique du moyen âge s'adressant spécialement aux femmes* (Cahors: Couselant, 1903), 55–7 (55).
33. Amos Parducci, *Costumi ornati: Studi sugli insegnamenti di cortigiana medievali* (Bologna: Zanichelli, 1928), 41–2 and 49.

34. Erich Müller, *Die altprovenzalische versnovelle* (Halle: Niemeyer, 1930), 102–9. (Müller wrote at a time before the capitalization of nouns was prescribed in German.)
35. Marc-René Jung, *Etudes sur le poème allégorique en France au moyen âge* (Berne: Franke, 1971), 148–59 (159).
36. Ibid. 154. Cf. Constans, *Manuscrits*, 115 n.
37. Don A. Monson, *Les 'ensenhamens' occitans: essai de définition et de délimitation du genre* (Paris: Klincksieck, 1981), 94–8.
38. Jones further discusses the *Cort d'Amor* in two articles: '*Lo Saber* dans les quatre allégories occitanes du XIIIe siècle', in *Studia Occitanica in memoriam Paul Remy*, ed. Hans-Erich Keller, 2 vols. (Kalamazoo: Michigan Medieval Institute, 1986), ii. 81–92; 'Narrative transformations of twelfth-century troubadour lyric', in *The Expansions and Transformations of Courtly Literature: Selected Papers from the Second Triennial Congress of the International Courtly Literature Society*, ed. N. B. Smith and J. T. Snow (Athens: Georgia University Press, 1980), 117–27. Robert Taylor, 'The figure of *Amor* in the Old Provençal narrative allegories', in *Court and Poet: Proceedings of the Third Congress of the International Courtly Literature Society*, ed. G. S. Burgess and others (Liverpool: Cairns, 1980), 309–17, also briefly considers our text, concluding that Amor is presented as a man.
39. Alfred Jeanroy, *Histoire sommaire de la poésie occitane des origines à la fin du XVIIIe siècle* (Toulouse: Privat, 1945), 84.
40. Robert Lafont and Christian Anatole, *Nouvelle Histoire de la littérature occitane*, Publications de l'institut d'études occitanes, 2 vols. (Bruges: Presses Universitaires de France, 1960–6), i. 120–1.
41. Giuseppe E. Sansone, *Testi didattico-cortesi di Provenza* (Bari: Adriatica, 1977), 7.
42. See Jacques Lafitte-Houssat, *Troubadours et cours d'amour* (Paris: Presses Universitaires de France, 1950), *passim*, and Paul Remy, 'Les "cours d'amour": légende et réalité', *Revue de l'université de Bruxelles* 7 (1954–5), 179–97.
43. For the knight and cleric debates, see (in Latin) the *Altercatio Phyllidis et Florae*: Patrick Gerard Walsh (ed.), *Love Lyrics from the Carmina Burana* (Chapel Hill: University of North Carolina Press, 1993), 101–10; (in Old French) the texts in Charles Oulmont, *Les Débats du clerc et du chevalier dans la littérature poétique du moyen âge* (Paris: Champion, 1911), and Edmond Faral, *Recherches sur les sources latines des contes et romans courtois du moyen âge* (Paris: Champion, 1913), 251–98.
44. Irville Charles Lecompte (ed.), 'Le Fablel dou Dieu d'Amors', *Modern Philology* 8 (1910), 63–86; Wendelin Foerster (ed.), *De Venus la Déesse d'Amour: Altfranzösisches Minnegedicht aus dem XIII. Jahrhundert* (Bonn: Cohen, 1880).
45. There is a Latin knight and cleric debate, the *Concilium Remiremontensis* (ed. Oulmont, *Les Débats*, 93–110) in which the whole text is devoted to the debate, but the Court of Love does not feature, the debate taking place in a convent. The *Roman de la Rose* is perhaps similarly focused on the Court of Love, but it is very consciously framed within a dream, and the dreamer has to enter the court.
46. Paul Zumthor, *Essai de poétique médiévale* (Paris: Seuil, 1972), 161: 'Les textes composés en octosyllabes narratifs relèvent de plusieurs discours entre lesquels on ne rencontre que peu de traits communs.'
47. Hans Robert Jauss, 'Theorie der Gattungen und Literatur des Mittelalters', in *Grundriss der romanischen Literaturen des Mittelalters*, ed. Hans Robert Jauss and Erich Köhler, 13 vols. (Heidelberg: Winter, 1968–72), i. 107–38 (114).

32 INTRODUCTION

48. Douglas Kelly, *The Art of Medieval French Romance* (Madison: University of Wisconsin Press, 1992), 318.
49. Patrick Gerard Walsh, *Andreas Capellanus on Love*, Duckworth Classical, Medieval and Renaissance Editions (London: Duckworth, 1982). This text is also sometimes known as *De arte honeste amandi*. The 21 judgements come in book 2, ch. 7 (pp. 250–71). I refer to the judgements by number.
50. Walsh expresses doubt as to the historical existence of courts of love, concluding 'if such a court did exist, it could only have been as an informal entertainment' (*Andreas Capellanus*, 155 n.).
51. For the Court of Love, see *De amore*, bk 1 ch. 6 (102–21).
52. The dating of Andreas Capellanus' work is itself a contentious matter, on which see Walsh, who nevertheless considers a date in the 1180s as quite likely (*Andreas Capellanus*, 1–2). If the two works can indeed be linked, we may assume much the same date of composition for the *Cort d'Amor*.
53. Jones, *Cort*, 17. Her examples have not been quoted here as they will be dealt with in what follows.
54. See Monson, *Ensenhamens*, 94–8 (on the *Cort d'Amor*) and *passim*.
55. Sansone, *Testi didattico-cortesi*, 58.
56. See Jones, *Cort*, 22–32 for full details of common elements.
57. Although these are reductionist definitions of courtly and Ovidian codes of love, they are still conveniently established and *grosso modo* correct.
58. Jung, *Etudes*, 154–5.
59. Failing to recognize the temporal sequence, Jung (*Etudes*, 149–51) and Jones (*Cort*, 70–2) have some difficulty reconciling the two.
60. As before, appreciating the sequential nature of the account obviates difficulties arising from seemingly opposing views such as a lady having not to sleep with her lover too soon (ll. 525–38) but enjoying coercion at a later stage (ll. 576–84), a contrast which Jones calls 'an unsolvable problem' (*Cort*, 26).
61. Ibid.
62. Jung, *Etudes*, 154–8.
63. Ibid. 158–9; Taylor, 'Figure', 312.
64. For a classic exposition of *amplificatio* as a rhetorical structure, see Alan Murray Finlay Gunn, *The Mirror of Love* (Lubbock: Texas Tech, 1952), 76–94.
65. Several scholars have commented on the glossatory function of Amor's instruction in the *Roman de la Rose*. For one such reading, see Hult, *Self-fulfilling Prophecies*, 176–8.
66. The *Cort d'Amor* thus fits into a tradition of early secular narrative allegory which engages with issues at stake in the universals debate. I examine that tradition in my thesis: 'The Emergence of Narrative Secular Allegory in Old French and Occitan before 1273', Ph.D. thesis (Cambridge, 1999). I hope to publish an extended version of my findings in the near future.
67. Proessa in fact initially describes himself as *entremessa* (l. 1335), so there is some ambiguity.
68. The character Male Bouche is female for the first 3000 lines or so, then consistently male. See Hult, *Self-fulfilling Prophecies*, 244 n., and Douglas Kelly, *Internal Difference and Meanings in the 'Roman de la Rose'* (Madison: University of Wisconsin Press, 1995), 108 ff. In the edition of Daniel Poirion, *Le Roman de la Rose* (Paris: Garnier Flammarion, 1974), Verité also undergoes syllepsis (cf. Sarah

Kay, *Subjectivity in Troubadour Poetry* (Cambridge: Cambridge University Press, 1990), 171–4). Although remaining grammatically male, Bel Acueil is addressed as though he were a woman: see Simon Gaunt, 'Bel Acueil and the improper allegory of the *Romance of the Rose*', *New Medieval Literatures* 2 (1998), 65–93.

69. This is the passage selected by Lavaud and Nelli for inclusion in their anthology, no doubt because of its literary quality.

EDITORIAL PRINCIPLES

❖

As a *unica*, the *Cort d'Amor* presents the editor with different problems from a work with multiple manuscript versions. If I have not had to choose between alternatives, I have not had any kind of 'control' text to look to in cases where this text seems corrupt. In fact, the *Cort d'Amor* presents a number of problems, not all of which I can claim to have resolved. In general, I have tried to correct the manuscript lesson as little as possible. However, although I am wary of providing a 'sanitized' text which is unrepresentative of the actual manuscript witness, I have found certain emendations desirable where there seem to be corruptions in the text. The whole purpose of a critical edition is, after all, to make the text more accessible to modern readers.

The division of words in the manuscript is erratic and generally speaking I have redivided lines without comment. Only where a line can be reorganized in more than one way (for instance, l. 29) do I add a note. In the manuscript, *c* and *t* are often so similar as to be indistinguishable, and the use of minims is also frequently unclear. My reading of the manuscript differs from the diplomatic editions of Mahn and Jones almost exclusively in such cases. Constans only saw the manuscript once, and as a result a number of misreadings are evident in his edition, including the omission of a whole line (l. 1458). (It is a tribute to the ingenuity and knowledge of Chabaneau that his proposed corrections more than once re-establish the actual manuscript lesson.) Although such misreadings are themselves an interesting illustration of how errors can be made in copying, I have generally not recorded them. Constans attributes line numbers to most of the lacunas in the text, with the result that from l. 904 onwards his line numbering differs from mine. As it is far from evident how many lines may have been omitted in each case, I prefer not to include the lacunas in my line numbering. Given that this leads to a difference of only nine lines by the end of the text, and to avoid confusion, I always refer to lines following my own numbering.

EDITORIAL PRINCIPLES 35

With the exception of Mahn and Jones, previous editors have attempted to standardize orthography and prosody. I have not recorded their modifications of orthography where they are purely cosmetic and do not affect the meaning. My own policy, as stated above, is to respect the manuscript lesson unless there is a compelling reason to emend. My aim is not to improve the style of the text, merely to render it more comprehensible. My policy on individual points of prosody, orthography, morphology, syntax, and translation and layout is outlined below. Rejected manuscript readings are recorded in footnotes. Problems, emendations, previous editors' solutions and any other critical commentary on the text or translation appear in the notes at the end of the text. Unusual words are discussed in the Glossary. As highlighted in the Introduction, there are a number of gallicisms in the text, indicating transmission in the north of France. Each case is dealt with in the note to the line in question and, for quick reference, all are collected together in a special section of the Glossary.

Prosody

The *Cort d'Amor* is written in rhyming octosyllabic couplets without caesurae. Unlike earlier editors, I do not assume that any metrical irregularities (i.e. more or less than eight syllables a line) are scribal and that the author never made such mistakes, or even considered such issues as crucial. I have taken irregular lines to constitute a suggestion, not an assurance, that there may be a corruption in the text. I do not emend on the basis of prosody alone. Thus for example, l. 30 (*sa gent Amors la dousa e la bona*) is maintained as it appears in the manuscript because it is grammatically and syntactically correct, even if it could easily be emended (*e·l bona*) to make it scan, whereas ll. 33–4 (*ab cui fai acorda[da]ment / d'amor lo lial zutgament*) merit the addition of the syllable *da* because the syntax is problematic without it. In instances where I have not corrected, the problem and any earlier editors' solutions are recorded in a note.

Although metrical irregularities are not uncommon in medieval verse, there is an unusually high proportion of them in this text: over 70 of the 1721 lines (over 4 per cent) as they stand in the manuscript do not have eight syllables. There are even more irregular lines if an indulgent attitude towards elision and hiatus is not adopted. There seems to have been a certain fluidity in the scansion of verses, so that syllables could be elided or not according to the practical needs of a performer. Thus in l. 16, for example (*que·l romanz deveda e castia*), the *e* needs to be elided with the preceding *a* for the scansion to work, whereas in l. 45 (*Bon'Esperancha e Paors*), there must be hiatus between the -*a* and the *e*. This is a common feature of medieval verse, but the same cannot be said of the disregard of the principle of using initial *h*- to indicate hiatus. On seven occasions (ll. 61, 83, 428, 489, 542, 1551, 1629), we find lines which only scan as octosyllabic if the *h*- is ignored and the vowels on either side are elided (for example l. 61: *e chascuna ha son amador*).

A similar phenomenon occurs with the word *enaissi* in l. 97. The full line is: *enaissi con deu far lo seingner*. Whilst the orthography of *enaissi* indicates a trisyllabic word, the metre of the line demands only two syllables and it is hard to see why the preferred orthography is not *aisi*, *ensins* or similar. These two features suggest that the version we have in Chansonnier *N* is several times removed from any performer's copy of the *Cort d'Amor*. (We do know that the *Cort d'Amor* was intended for performance from *auzatz* in l. 5. There is no evidence that narrative works existed on song sheets, in the way that lyric poems are generally thought to have done, but by 'performer's copy' I simply mean any copy that was used for oral performance.) Metrical irregularities are essentially offences against the ear, not the eye, and it is unlikely that anyone writing with a performance in mind would complicate a performer's task unnecessarily by writing superfluous letters which undermine regular scansion. Once the transmission of the text is primarily through the written medium, however, precise syllable count becomes less important, and this might explain the profusion of irregular lines throughout the text.

A move from oral to written transmission is not, however, sufficient in itself to explain so many irregularities. Many romances for which we possess much less evidence of performance are much more regular in their scansion. Perhaps, given that our manuscript witness is a mid- to late thirteenth-century Italian copy of a late twelfth-century work which shows linguistic evidence of circulation in northern France, we can presume that on one occasion, if not several, the text was copied by someone who was not very familiar with Occitan. It seems reasonable to assume that mistakes are more likely to creep in when scribes are not using their own language. Whatever the exact details are, however, we must accept that this text has been carelessly copied by one or more scribes. Of course, we cannot prove that the author was punctilious when it came to metre, but the evidence of the superfluous initial *h* and *enaissi* points to scribal error. I do not believe, finally, that the metrical irregularities in our text are the result of a translation. For one thing, most of those irregularities could easily be ironed out; for another, despite the disregard for strict metre, the text as we have it is undoubtedly written in elegant and frequently complex Occitan.

Orthography

The first letter of each line has not been capitalized. The use of capitals in this position is entirely arbitrary in the manuscript and for facility of reading I have preferred to follow syntax alone in this respect. As far as the capitalization of personifications is concerned, I follow tradition by capitalizing in cases where the noun governs a verb or is given attributes which suggest human-like agency or status. I believe this facilitates reading, although it does also tend to obviate ambiguity, which is a central theme of this text. Medieval manuscripts do not highlight personifications in this way, although this text is remarkable for using the very gender of *amor* to signal personification (on which, see my Introduction).

Abbreviations in the manuscript have been expanded without being marked as such. Any potential ambiguities arising from abbreviations are discussed in the notes. Additions are marked in square brackets: [ ], expunctuations in parentheses: ( ). Where the manuscript lesson has been replaced by a correction, the correction is underlined and the original appears in a footnote. The one exception to this is the correction of final *-j/-z* to *-i*. I follow this convention and record the MS lesson, but do not underline the *-i*.

A feature of the text is the letter *z* in instances where other graphemes are more usually found: *g-* (l. 1045), *-r* (ll. 453, 843), *-s* (l. 204), *-tz* (ll. 622, 1476), *-ssa* (l. 1271 *-sza*), *i* (ll. 12, 32, 33 etc.) and *j* (ll. 9, 28, 29 etc.). This is a contribution of the Italian scribe, and has not been altered except to follow the convention of final *-i* after a vowel (similarly final *-j*, *j* on its own and *lj / jl* become *-i*, *i*, *li*, *il*) for ease of reading.

Given the fluidity of medieval orthography, it is sometimes difficult to distinguish an idiosyncratic spelling from a scribal error. I maintain the manuscript lesson unless a form is contrary to the rules of etymology. Thus a form like *seigna* (l. 154) is maintained, whereas *nue(t)it* (l. 330) is emended. Unusual spellings of common words are discussed in the notes, whilst unusual words are discussed in the Glossary.

Morphology

Like other medieval romance languages, Occitan experienced a long period of transition from being an analytic to a synthetic language. This text shows evidence of past participles which are sometimes inflected, sometimes not; *lur* as a pronoun or possessive adjective remains invariable, as is common in the classical period of troubadour poetry, except on three occasions as a possessive adjective (ll. 24, 399, 751—my emendation removes one of the two manuscript instances in l. 399) when it takes an inflectional -*s* in the plural. Elsewhere (ll. 332, 335, 784, 817, 1062, 1622, 1628, 1684) we find uninflected *lur* as a plural possessive adjective. I have not attempted to standardize either of these elements.

The use of -*s* as an inflexional ending on masculine substantives and adjectives is also quite irregular in this text. During the Middle Ages, the language as a whole moved from using -*s* to indicate subject case singulars and object case plurals to indicating only plurals in either case. Yet we find numerous examples of 'incorrect' forms (in the feminine as well) which cannot be explained by this shift. This is common, even in quite early texts, and can no doubt be explained by assimilation, as well as scribal error, but I have chosen to standardize these inflexional endings (to the older, bicasual system, which is well observed elsewhere in the text) in order to facilitate reading. Some of the irregularities have implications for personification, and these are dealt with in the notes.

Unstable -*n* has not been added in final position (ll. 412, 528, 550 etc.), nor in (rarer) middle position by assimilation (ll. 434 and 859 *matenant*, 564 *lausamet*, 1012 *coven*, 1313 *gras*, 1343 *avetura*, 1669 *retegutz*, 1696 *vejansa*). These could simply be the result of the omission of abbreviation marks. Comparison with the translation will clarify any ambiguities.

Syntax and Translation

As I have used English syntax as a guide to punctuating the text, my punctuation is frequently different from that of Constans. Only in cases where this significantly alters the meaning have I signalled it.

Occitan had no strict rules on sequence of tenses. I have not imposed modern English sequence of tenses on the edition, but I have on the translation in order to avoid unnecessary inelegance. The one exception is the frequent alternation of narrative past and lyric present tenses, which I have retained. Otherwise, I privilege the source text in my translation. My aim is to give the non-specialist the clearest possible idea of exactly *what* is said. Square brackets in the translation indicate clarifications or something added to help the English style.

Jones's (diplomatic) edition of the text is generally accurate. Unfortunately, the same cannot be said of her translation. To record all differences between her translation and mine would take an inordinate amount of space and would rapidly become more churlish than simply drawing a veil thereover. In any case, her edition, unlike that of Constans, is still readily available to anyone desiring to consult it.

Layout

The *Cort d'Amor* occupies section 5, folios 31^r to 46^v, of the manuscript. It is preceded by a blank folio and a blank page and comes between the anonymous poem *Bona dompna pros ez onrada* and a poem by Aimeric de Peguillan, *Qui la vi, en ditz*. Two of the five hands identified in N copied the *Cort d'Amor*: one from folios 31^r to 35^v, and the other from 35^v to 46^v. Up to and including our text the poems are copied one line of verse per line of manuscript; following our text the verses are copied continuously. There are two columns of text per page. Spaces have been left for a miniature and initials, which sadly were never executed. The *Cort d'Amor* is incomplete at the end and breaks off at the very bottom of the second column of folio 46^v; as I have only seen the manuscript on film I cannot say if the loss of the ending might be the result of the division of quires.

In my edition I have indented lines which are indented in the manuscript for the never-executed miniature and initials. Usually two lines are indented, but on several occasions only one. This is no doubt indicative of the size of the initial to be drawn. To enable the quickest possible comparison between the source text and my translation, I have positioned the latter facing the former and similarly organized in verses. Wherever possible I have tried to position each line of the translation directly opposite the corresponding line of the source text, but the non-specialist reader should be aware that in some cases syntax has demanded a reorganization of line order in the translation. There are several cases of enjambment, and I have endeavoured to retain them, even when it has proved necessary to link the lines using different elements from the source text.

Text and Translation

LA CORT D'AMOR

❖

[S]einor, vos que volez la flor *fol. 31ʳ col. 1*
e la corteszia d'amor,
e non avetz soing d'autr'aver
mas ab ioi voletz remaner,
5 auzatz un romanz bon e bel
bastit de ioi fin e novel.
E gardatz quant l'auresz auszit,
non metatz los motz en oblit.
Que za negus hom no fara
10 so que·l romanz comandara,
no sia plens de corteszia
e que non guerrei* villania.
Que lo be que lo romanz di
fasson las dompnas e·l drut fi
15 e gardon se de la folia
que·l romanz deveda e castia.
Que vos sabetz qu'ab desmeszura
perd Amors a tor[t] ssa dreitura,
que Malvestat e Putaria
20 no·l laisson tener dreita via.
Per so han fag novella amor
d'una domna de gran valor *col. 2*
viij.xx. que donas qe pulsellas,
q'an trobat lurs raszons novellas
25 coment amors sia lials.
Fuguon s'en las falsas e·ls fals,
q'a tant Amors parlament
no·s taingha za* galiament.
Ora zuzatz* coment araszona
30 sa gent Amors la dousa e la bona.

12 MS *guerrez*   28 MS *taing ha za*   29 MS *or azuzatz*

THE COURT OF LOVE

❖

My lords, you who desire the flower
and the courtliness of love,
and have no care for other wealth
but wish to abide with joy,
5 hear a good and beautiful romance
composed of fine new joy.
And mind that when you have heard it
you do not forget the words.
For never will any man do
10 that which the romance ordains
if he is not full of courtliness
and does not wage war on uncouthness.
Let ladies and faithful lovers
do the good which the romance prescribes
15 and keep themselves from the folly
which the romance forbids and censures.
For you know that with excess
Love wrongly loses that which is his right,
because Wickedness and Licentiousness
20 do not let him follow the right path.
Which is why eight score ladies and maidens,
have made a new [type of] love [/Love]
for [/out of] a lady of great merit,
and they have invented new arguments
25 [as to] how love [/Love] can be legitimate [/loyal].
Let false men and women flee from that place,
for Love holds such an assembly
that deceit is certainly not fitting.
Now judge how 'Lady' Love the sweet and good
30 addresses his people.

Mas premieramens vos dirai
sos conpainons, ni hon estai*,
ab cui fai* acorda[da]ment
d'amor lo lial zutgament.
35 [E]l temps q'el roissignol faz nausa
qe de nueit ni de zor no pausa
desots la fuella de cantar
pel bel temps que vei refrescar,
aven que Fin'Amors parlet
40 ab sos barons en son rescet
en som del Puei de Parnasus.
Zoi e Solasz foron lai sus
e Ardimens e Corteszia
qe de flors l'enzonchon la via.
45 Bon'Esperancha e Paors
li portent de denant las flors.
D'autra part Larguesza e Domneis
lo meton en un leit d'orfreis.
Celars e Dousa Conpania   fol. 31ᵛ col. 1
50 geton desus ruesa floria*.
Le cortes pueih de l'autra part
del Fuoch d'Amor relusz ez art.
D'aqui mou tota la ioza
qu'Amors permei* lo mond envoza.
55 E d'autra part son las floretas:
la[s] ruosas e las violetas,
qi trameton lor gran douszor
devant lo leit de Fin'Amor.
E d'autra part ha cent pulsellas,
60 q'anc negus hom non vi plus bellas,
e chascuna ha son amador
e son vestu d'una color.
Baison ez [a]braisson soven
e mantenon pretz e ioven;
65 totz temps han aital desdug
a d'aital gen vai be, so cug.
E d'autra part hac un ombrage
on hac maint auzel saulvatge

---

32 MS *estaz*   33 MS *faz*   50 MS *desus idesa floria*   54 MS *permez*

            But first I will tell you
            who his companions are, and where he is,
            with whom he jointly makes
            the lawful judgement of love.
35   In the time when the nightingale breaks into
            sound, when he pauses neither night nor day
            from singing beneath the leaf
            because of the beautiful season I see renewing itself,
            it happens that True Love spoke
40   with his barons in his retreat
            on the top of Mount Parnassus.
            Joy and Conversation were up there
            and Courage and Courtliness
            who strew the road with flowers for him.
45   Good Hope and Fear
            bring the flowers into his presence.
            In another place Largesse and Love Service
            place him in a bed of gold cloth.
            Discretion and Sweet Company
50   strew fully-blossomed roses over it.
            The courtly mountain, in another place,
            shines and burns with the Fire of Love.
            From here originates all the joy
            which Love sends out throughout the world.
55   And in another place are the little flowers:
            the roses and the violets,
            who exude their great sweetness
            before the bed of True Love.
            And elsewhere there are a hundred maidens,
60   such that no man ever saw more beautiful ones,
            and each has her lover,
            and they are all dressed in the same colour.
            They kiss and embrace often
            and maintain worth and youth;
65   they have such pleasure the whole time [as]
            befits such people, so I think.
            And in another place there was a shady spot
            where there were many wild birds

que cantent la nueit e lo zor
70 voltas e lais de gran dousor.
Ez el mei loc ac un castel,
q'anc negus om non vi plus bel,
qe non ha una peira el mur
non luisza con d'aur o d'azur;
75 d'aqi guerezon Vilania.
Las claus son Pretz e Drudaria,   *col. 2*
e·l gaita q'es el castel cria:
'Esta lo drutz contra s'amia
e l'amia contra son drut.
80 Era non sera ia sauput,
ar es lo luochs e la saiszos,
qu'ieu hai* endormitz los gilos.'
Davant la porta hac una font,
e non a tan bella el mont,
85 qi sortz en una conca d'aur.
De tot le mont val le tesaur.
N'a om el mont, si n'a begut,
que, cant qe es e cant [qe] fut,
non sapchza de be e d'onor,
90 qe non oblit ira e dolor.
Claus'es de laurie[r]s e de pis
e de pomiers de paradis.
De flor(s) de lizs es coronada,
que nais menudet en la prada.
95 Aqi s'asis a parlament
Amors, e parlet bellament
enaissi con deu far lo seingner
qe tot lo mont ha a destreigner.
Esgardet vas terra un petit,
100 con sabis om, e pueis ha dit:
   'Seinors, eu me lau be de vos,
mas vos sabetz qe totz om pros
deu gardar q'en sa seinoria   *fol. 32ʳ col. 1*
fassa om sen e lais folia.
105 Qe vos sabetz q'ad obs d'amar
no val re[s] que vol folleiar.

      who night and day sing
70   songs and lays of great sweetness.
      And in the middle of the place there was a castle
      such that no man ever saw a more beautiful one,
      for there is not one stone in the walls
      which does not shine with gold or azure;
75   from here they wage war on Uncouthness.
      The keys are Worth and Courtship,
      and the watchman who is in the castle cries:
      'Let the lover be next to his lady
      and the lady next to her lover.
80   Now it [their love] will certainly not be known,
      now is the place and the time,
      for I have sent the jealous ones to sleep.'
      In front of the gate there was a fountain,
      and there is not such a beautiful one in the [whole] world,
85   which flows into a golden shell.
      It is worth all the treasure in the world.
      There is no man who, having drunk from it,
      does not know all there is and all there [ever] was
      to do with good and honour,
90   and who does not forget anger and sorrow.
      It is surrounded by laurels and pines
      and apple trees of paradise.
      It is crowned with lilies,
      which grow all over the meadow.
95   Here Love sat in session
      and spoke beautifully
      as should the lord
      who has the whole world to rule.
      He looked at the ground a little,
100 like a wise man, and then said:
         'My lords, I am very pleased with you,
      but you know that every worthy man
      must mind that under his lordship
      one does that which is judicious and leaves folly alone.
105 For you know that when it comes to love
      anyone who wishes to behave foolishly is worthless.

Que l'autrer nos dis Iohanitz,
que leon(s) aucis la formitz.
Don Iois, aisso dig contra vos:
110 que vos faitz aitant fort ioios
us vassal qe no er cellatz
si domna li fai sos agratz,
s'ia el non s'en vanara,
e lo blasme li remanra.
115 Vec vos la fromitz e·l leon:
la domna es morta pel garchon.
Eu·s comanc: non fassatz mais re
mas donatz zoi lai on conve:
als enfantz fatz con ad enfans,
120 als parladors donatz parlans;
e metatz en tot tal meszura
q'eu no i perda ma dreitura.
Que pros om i a grand onor
qan fai be l'afar son seinor.'
125 [A]pres araiszonet Solaz.
Tota la cort estet en paz.
'Seinor, mout si deur'om sofrir,
qe mout deu om son cors cobrir
qe non diga tot son coratge
130 ni non mostre grand alegratge, *col. 2*
mas lai on es luechs e meszura,
q'amors per be cellar meillura.
Qe l'auzel[s], cant el ve lo latz,
s'en fui d'aqi tost e viatz.
135 Tot altretal fai demanes
vilans qant ve(i) ome cortes
que viu de ioi e de solatz,
e porta trezador ni laz:
quant el lo ve, serra sa porta
140 e sa moiller es pesz qu'a morta.
Aisso dic per vos, Don Solatz,
qu'es mos amig[s] e mos privatz
ez affi vos la mia fe,
q'e tot lo mond non am tan re.
145 Mas voill qe laissetz la gaiessa
qan non ez luechs qe, si be·us pesa,

For Iohanitz recently told us
that the ant killed the lion.
Lord Joy, this is what I reproach you for:
110 that you make a man who will
not be discreet if a lady grants him
his desires just as very joyful
[as] if he does not boast about it,
and the blame will still attach to her.
115 Consider the ant and the lion:
the knave brings about the woman's death.
I command this: never do anything
but bestow joy there where it is fitting:
treat children like children,
120 give the speakers a place to speak;
and in all things place such moderation
that I may not lose my jurisdiction through it.
For a worthy man has great honour
when he conducts his lord's business well.'
125   Then he addressed Conversation.
    All the court remained silent.
'My lord, a man ought often to suffer thus,
because he often has to restrain himself
so that he does not relate all his feelings
130 nor show great happiness,
except there where it is opportune and reasonable,
for love improves through discretion.
For the bird, when he sees the trap,
flees from there quickly and without delay.
135 A churl immediately behaves in the
same way when he sees a courtly man
who lives with joy and conversation,
and carries a lure and a trap:
when he [the churl] sees him he [the churl] shuts his door
140 and his wife is worse than dead.
This I say to you, Lord Conversation,
who are my friend and confidant
and I assure you of my good faith,
for in all the world I love nothing so much [as you].
145 But I want you to abandon gaiety when it
is out of place for, even if it upsets you,

vos ensegnarai vostre pro.
Qar eu n'ai fort bel gaszardo
qe vos faitz amors comenssar,
150　vos faitz l'un a l'autre agradar,
vos non voletz enuei ni plors.
Viulas, dansas e tanbors
e Ioventz vos fan compania.
Seigna vos qi no sab la via
155　d'Amor, qe vos lo metretz lai
on om non meiss_o_na* mas iai.'
　　[A]pres parlet ab Ardiment:　　　　　　　　　　*fol. 32ᵛ col. 1*
'De vos me lau eu ben e gent
que vos faiz toszeta ardida,
160　q'a paors neis d'aucel qant crida.
Pueis la fasse(i)tz vos tant segura
q'a son drut vai* de nueit oscura
qe non tem marit ne parent
batre ni menassar sovent.
165　E faitz a paubre drut enqerre
domna q'a gran fieu e gran terre.
Qe·l ditz: "Se no·m laissas estar,
eu te farai ton enuei far".
E cel, que de re non s'esfreda,
170　sitot s'a petit de moneda
s'adoba ades de ben servir.
Pueis la fatz tant enardir
qu'ela oblida son lignatje,
sa riqesa e son paraie,
175　e torna tot son cor en lui;
e son bon amic ambedui*.
E per vos vai a parlament
drutz a si donz ardi[da]ment.
En amor non val re paors:
180　ardiments es la claus d'amors.
　　[C]ortesia, de vos non sai
dir [totz] lo[s] bens qe de vos hai,
ni non sai grazir las onors
q'ieu hai de vos, ni las lauszors.　　　　　　　　　　*col. 2*

156 MS *meissarna*　　162 MS *vaz*　　176 MS *ambeduz*

The Court of Love 51

  I will show you [how it can be to] your advantage.
  For I reap a very great reward
  because you make love relationships begin,
150 you make the one agreeable to the other,
  you do not desire anxiety or tears.
  Viols, dances and tambours
  and Youth keep you company.
  Instruct anyone who does not know the pathway
155 of Love, so that you may install him there
  where one harvests nothing but joy.'
   Then he spoke with Boldness:
   'With you I am well and nobly pleased
  for you embolden the young girl
160 who is even afraid of the bird when it chirps.
  Then make her so secure
  that she goes to her lover in the thick of night
  and fears from husband or relative neither
  regular beating nor threats.
165 And you make the poor lover seek
  a lady who has a large fief and extensive lands.
  For she says to him: "If you do not leave me alone,
  I will have that done which is to your disadvantage".
  And he, who is not afraid of anything,
170 even though he has little money
  immediately sets about serving her well.
  Then you make her so bold
  that she forgets her lineage,
  her rank and her birth,
175 and she turns her whole heart to him;
  and they love each other dearly.
  And through you the lover boldly
  goes to speak with his lady.
  In love fear is worth nothing:
180 boldness is the key to love relationships.
   Courtliness, about you I cannot
   say what good things I have on your account,
  nor can I thank you for the honours
  that I have on your account, nor the praises.

52   La Cort d'Amor

185 Q'ab plana razon de sofrir
me fatz a tot(z) mon abellir.
Ab lo sofrir avetz mesura,
per qe vostre bon pretz meillura.
Vos metetz mesura en parlar.
190 Enuei* no sabetz vos ia far,
ni ia negus om non er pros
si non ha compania ab vos,
que aqel que i a compania
non fara orguoill ni follia.
195 [B]on'Esperansa, grand aiuda
me fatz qar vostre cor no·s muda.
Q'al premier que vol faire druda,
el ven a leis, si la saluda
e pueis comensa la pregar,
200 per Deu, q'ella lo deia amar.
Bon'Esperansa la lo guida
e sitot noncha l'es gracida
sa pregueira al comensar,
ades lo faz ben esperar.
205 Qe greu verreis novella amia
q'a premier non se fassa enia.
Qe·l dira: "Ges no·us amarai!"*
"Domna, per qe?" "Q'altr'amic hai."
o dira: "Ges no·us amaria,
210 q'onor e marit en perdria".
O dira qe: "Plen ses d'engan,   *fol. 33ʳ col. 1*
vos amador per qe·us soan".
Bon'Esperansa ditz c'aison
non cal tot prezar* un boton
215 qant el se desditz ne s'orguella,
q'adoncs se descausa e despuella.

190 MS *enuez*
207–8 I have inverted ll. 207 and 208. The order in which they appear in
the manuscript seems to be incorrect since there is nothing to introduce
the direct speech in (my) l. 208. Also, '*Domna, per qe?*' (in my l. 208) only
makes sense as a response to a statement such as that from the lady in (my)
l. 207. Other editions do not invert these lines, although Constans does
comment that (his and the manuscript's) l. 207 is a 'vers obscur'.
214 MS *preiar*

185 For simply by giving me cause to suffer,
you make me praised throughout the world.
With suffering you have moderation,
through which your good worth improves.
You endow speech with moderation.
190 You certainly cannot ever cause irritation,
nor will any man ever be worthy
if he does not keep company with you,
for he who keeps such company
will not do that which is proud or foolish.
195   Good Hope, great assistance
you give me since your heart does not change.
For when he [a lover] first wants to make
someone his beloved, he comes and greets her
and then begins to implore her,
200 for God's sake, that she should love him.
Good Hope leads him there
and although his prayer is never
granted to him at the beginning,
you immediately make him hope keenly [/hope for a reward].
205 For you will scarcely see a new lady-love
who does not appear annoyed at first.
And she will say to him: "I will definitely not love you",
"Lady, why?" "Because I have another lover."
or she will say: "I will not love you at all
210 for I would lose honour and husband through it".
Or she will say: "You are full of deceit,
you lovers, which is why I despise you".
Good Hope says that there is no need to
value this as much as a button
215 when she refuses him and becomes proud,
for straight afterwards she is taking off her shoes and clothes.

[P]aors, vos siatz benedeita.
Per vos vai drutz la via dreita,
qe qant vai a si dons parlar,
220 q'el li cuida desmostrar,
e dire, qe per s'amor mor
e vos li donatz ins el cor
si q'el non sab dire razo,
ni sab detriar oc ni no.
225 Qe qant ha trestot iorn parlat,
non cuia aver dit mas foudat,
e qant l'a trames son message,
et el pensa en son corage:
"Las! Aiso·l mandetz solamen.
230 Ben sabra q'eu hai pauch de sen.
Jamais non virara sol l'uel:
aiso se tenra az orguel.
Catieu! Qe faras si·t soana
o si tos messages t'engana?
235 O qe faras si desir lonia,
o·l messages te dis mensonia?
Ben sa[be]z qe m'esca[r]nara
e mon message me batra.
Non fara qe tan es cortesa,
240 ja non fara aital malesa!
Caitieu! Mala la vi'enanch.
Sa plaia me tol tot lo sanch.
Be·m pesa qar lo i ai trames,
que sos maritz es mala res.
245 E dieus, co m'aura vergoinat,
si mon message auci ni bat!"
Aici vos dic on nos estem:
Re non ama om qe non tem.
  [L]argueza, vos voell castiar,
250 e si·m fatz vos tot mon afar.
Qe greu pot haver gran proesa
negus om si non ha larguesa;
ni causa no pot om trobar
qi tant vailla ad obs d'amar.

Fear, may you be blessed.
Through you the lover follows the just path,
for when he goes to talk to his lady,
220 for he thinks he will show her,
and say, that he is dying for her love,
then deep in his heart you make him
unable to say his piece
and unable to tell between yes and no.
225 So that when he has been speaking the whole day
he does not believe he has spoken anything but folly
and when he has sent her his messenger
he nevertheless thinks in his heart:
"Alas! Only this have you sent her.
230 Well will she know that I have little judgement.
She will never so much as cast a glance in my direction:
she will inwardly consider this to be pride [on my part].
Miserable wretch! What will you do if she spurns you,
or if your messenger deceives you?
235 Or what will you do if she keeps desire distant
or the messenger tells you lies?
Well you know that she will mock me
and will beat my messenger on my account.
She will not do it for she is so courtly,
240 indeed she will never do such a wrong.
Miserable wretch! The road ahead is difficult.
The wound inflicted by her takes all my blood away.
It weighs upon me greatly that I have sent him there,
for her husband is a wicked creature.
245 Oh God! How he will have shamed me
if he kills or beats my messenger!"
I tell you here where we are:
A man who fears nothing, loves nothing.
    Largess, you I wish to instruct,
250 even if you [already] conduct all my business for me.
For a man can hardly have merit
if he does not have largess;
nor can one find anything
which is worth so much when it comes to love.

56 LA CORT D'AMOR

255 Mais no'scell* qe vostra proesa
meta·s en orba Cobet[ze]sa;
ni'scell* qe dones largament
a neguna dompna qe·s vent.
Qe qant il vos atrai ni·us tira,
260 ni del cor de preon sospira,
il non o fai mas feintament
per so que·l dones de l'argent.
E·l iois, qan cobeesa aiuda,
non es res mas amor venduda.
265 Per q'ieu vos prec qe·l fals sospir   *fol. 33^v col. 1*
no·us puoscan l'aver escotir,
mais qant veires domna de pretz,
digas li vos eissa in privetz
qe si·l donas, il vos dara
270 e de confundre·us gardara,
e pueis dara vos largament
joi* e proesa e ardiment.
  [D]omneis, qui·us vol mal sia onitz.
Per vos vai paubres drut[z] garnitz,
275 e vai en uvern a la bisa
qe non ha freig en sa camisa,
e conten se plus bellament
qe tals qe ha trop mais d'argent.
E c'el es richs, el fara cort
280 e torneiament e beort,
e parla[ra] plus bellament
ab lo paubre q'ab lo manent,
per so qe chadaüs om diga
ben de lui a sa dousa amiga.
285   [C]elamens, vos es la flors
don nais e creis lo ioi* d'amors.
Vos non voles enuei ni bruda,
ni ia domna no er batuda
per re qe* vos digatz en fol.
290 Vos non li viratz sol lo col

255 MS *noncell*   257 MS *nincell*   272 MS *joz*
286 MS *ioz*   289 MS *qi*

255 But I do not teach that your merit
should have anything to do with blind Covetousness;
nor do I instruct that you should give generously
to any woman who sells herself.
For when she attracts you and draws you close
260 and sighs from the bottom of her heart,
she does not do it but by pretence
so that you may give her money.
And joy, when covetousness supports it,
is nothing but sold love.
265 Which is why I beseech you that the false sighs
may not rob you of your wealth,
but when you see a lady of worth,
you yourself may say to her in private
that if you give to her, she shall give to you
270 and shall keep you from perishing,
and then she will generously give you
joy and merit and boldness.
    Love Service, let whoever wishes you ill be dishonoured.
    Through you the poor lover goes equipped
275 and goes around in winter in the north wind
and is not cold in [only] his shirt,
and conducts himself more handsomely
than one who has much more money.
And if he is rich, he shall hold court
280 and tournament and joust
and shall speak more handsomely
with the poor man than with the rich,
so that everyone may speak
well of him to his sweet lady-love.
285   Discretion, you yourself are the flower
    from which springs and grows the joy of love relationships.
You desire neither irritation nor gossip,
nor will a lady ever be beaten
through anything that you might say foolishly.
290 You do not turn even your head towards her

qant om o ve, ni fatz semblant
qe de ren mens aiatz* calant.
E qant es la sasons ni·l locs
vos fatz pareiser vostre[s] iocs.
295 Qan es partitz, cuza cascus
qe siatz monges ou resclus.
Vos voletz vostre ioi en pasz,
vos mantenes Ioi e Solasz.
Per Cortesia e per Onor,
300 vos doin la baneira d'Amor.
[D]olsa Compaina, fina druda
es soven per vos ben venguda,
e cela re a qi* plus li platz:
son bel amic entre sos bratz.
305 E·l baisza mil ves en la boca,
qe qant sos bel[s] cors al sieu toca
ella li ditz per plan solaz:
"Amics, enueia vos mos braz?"
El li respon: "Domna, el non!
310 Tan qan vos mi faitz m'es tan bon,
m'arma, mos cors, so m'es avis,
es el mei luec de Paradis!"
"Bels amics coindes e ioios,
si eu ren vaill, so es per vos,
315 q'anch Galvains ni Soredamors,
ni anch Floris ni Blanchaflors,
ni l'amors Ysolt ni Tristan,
contra nos dos non valg un gan."
"Bella domna, tant qant viurai,
320 sachas de fi vos servirai.
Q'ieu non voell qe a mort ni a vida
la nostra amors sia partida."
E volrion mais esser mort
q'entre lor agues un descort.
325 [D]rudaria, vos es dons Pres,
qe del castel las claus tenes.
Gardas qe s'aqest dez baron
vos aduiszon negun preszon,

292 MS *alatz*   303 MS *cela res qi*

when someone is watching, nor do you show
that you care at all for her.
And when it is the [right] time and place
you let your games show openly.
295 When you have gone, everyone thinks
that you are a monk or a hermit.
You desire your joy in peace,
you maintain Joy and Conversation.
For Courtliness and for Honour,
300 I give you the standard of Love.
 Sweet Company, a fine lady-love
 is often welcomed through you,
and [also through you] she has that thing which pleases her most:
her handsome lover in her arms.
305 And she kisses him a thousand times on the mouth,
and when her beautiful body touches his,
she says to him for the sheer pleasure of conversation:
"My love, do you mind being in my arms?"
And he replies to her: "Certainly not, my lady!
310 All that you do to me is so pleasing to me,
it seems to me that my soul and my body
are in the middle of Paradise!"
"My handsome lover, you who are charming and joyful,
if I am worth anything, it is through you,
315 for never Gawain and Soredamors,
nor ever Floris and Blancheflors,
nor the love of Isolde and Tristan,
were worth a glove compared to the two of us."
"Beautiful lady, for as long as I shall live,
320 know that I will serve you faithfully.
For, living or dead, I do not wish
our love to be divided."
And they would rather be dead
than that there should be a disagreement between them.
325 Courtship, you are the lady of Merit
 for you hold the keys of the castle.
Mind that if these ten barons
bring you any prisoner,

qe lo metas en Fuec d'Amor,
330 gardan [lo] la nue(t)it e lo zor.
E zamais non haion be
tro lor domnas n'aion merce.
Si prenon domnas dos tans plus fort,
las conduisetz trus q'a la mort
335 tro qez mandon a lur amics
qe non lor aion cor enics.
Qe fort fers* deu om tormentar
las domnas car se fan pregar.
E si chai venon amador,
340 domnas ni drutz de gran valor,
e vos lo[r] fatz fort bel ostal,
asetzes los al deis rial
e colgas los lai dins la tor
en la mia cambra de flor.'
345 [Q]ant Amors hac s'a gran leszer
comandat e dit son plaszer,   *col. 2*
las domnas l'an ben autreiat,
qe d'aco qe ha comandat
li faran de tot son talan,
350 qe ia mot non traspassaran.
Mais de leis volrion saber
q'al amor deu hom mais tener.
E preigan lo com lor seignor
q'el las engart de desonor
355 qe tant pros domnas com ellas son
non haion blasme per lo mon,
ni qe lor pretz ni lor valor
non lur destrua Fals'Amor,
e qe lur diga soltiment,
360 per razon e per iugament,
so qe fai d'amor a gardar,
e aco q'hom en dei'ostar.
[S]o dis Amors: 'Bon conseil sai:
Na Corteszia, q'eu vei* lai.
365 Voell qe·m fassa aqest iutgament,
qe sab per on monta e disent

337 MS *sers*   364 MS *vez*

that you put him in the Fire of Love,
330 guarding him night and day.
And may they never have peace
until their ladies are merciful.
If they take ladies twice as strong,
lead them [those ladies] to death itself
335 until they assure their lovers
that they do not have an ill-disposed heart toward them.
For one must torment ladies very
fiercely because they demand to be beseeched.
And if lovers come here,
340 ladies and lovers of great worth,
and you give them a very fine lodging,
seat them at the royal table
and give them a bed there in the tower
in my flower room.'
345   When Love, greatly at his leisure, had
commanded this and said what would please him,
the ladies swore to him truly
that concerning that which he commanded,
they would do his pleasure for him in everything,
350 that they would never disobey a word [of it].
But they would like to know of the laws
which one must abide by the most in love.
And they beseech him as their lord
that he keep them from dishonour
355 in order that such worthy ladies as they are
may not be condemned throughout the world,
and that False Love may destroy
neither their reputation nor their merit,
and that he tell them subtly,
360 through reason and through judgement,
what of love it is fitting to retain,
and what one should reject.
   Thus spoke Love: 'I know a good adviser:
Lady Courtliness, whom I see there.
365 I want her to make this judgement for me,
for she knows through what love is augmented and

amors, e qar sab ben q'il es
del mont la plus adreita res,
il le fera be ses engan.'
370 Corteszia pleigua son gan
e [a]doba se de iugar
(q'om cortes se fai pauch pregar
qant ve(i) q'ez luecs es avinents). *fol. 34^V col. 1*
Molt es grantz e preon[s] sos sens.
375 Puis parlet com savis e pros.
Gent font auszida sa[s] razos.
'[S]einors, per dreig e per usage
deu Amors gardar son parage.
Qe paubrezta ab gentilesa
380 val mais q'orgueill ab riquesa.
Ni a sa cort non ai·n res at,
mais servir ab humilitat.
Eu vos o dirai ben e bon,
e breuiar vos hai la raszon.
385 Fin'Amors es de qatre res:
La premiera es bona fes;
e la cegon[d]a* lialtatz,
e sos afars sia cellatz;
e la terza si es mesura,
390 de parlar per la g[e]nt tafura;
e la qarta sapchas es sens,
ab q'Amors fai tots sos talens.
Aqesta devem mantener
e gardar de nostre poder.
395 Mais la falsa via bastarsa
qe sec la gent q'el fuec fos arsa,
las traïritz e las venals,
las camzaritz e las comunals
(que las femm(e)n[a]s e lors amors,*
400 es tot chaitiviers e dolors), *col. 2*

387 MS *cegōna*. The redundant horizontal bar over the *o* in the manuscript suggests that the *n* should, in fact, have been another letter, i.e. *d*.
399 MS *que lor femēs elors amors*

diminished, and because well she knows that it is
the most just thing in the world,
she will do it well and without deceit.'
370 Courtliness clasped his [Love's] glove
and prepared to make the judgement
(for the courtly man needs little beseeching
when he sees it is meet and seemly).
Her judgement is great and profound.
375 Then she spoke like a wise and worthy person.
Her arguments were keenly heard.
   'My lords, by right and by custom,
   Love must pay attention to his good breeding.
For poverty with good breeding
380 is worth more than pride with wealth.
Nor, at his court, do I need anything
but to serve with humility.
I will tell you this well and truly,
and I will summarize the argument for you.
385 True Love is made of four things:
The first is good faith;
and the second loyalty,
and that his business should be hidden;
and the third is restraint
390 from speaking amongst base people;
and know that the fourth is judgement,
with which Love achieves all his desires.
This we must maintain
and mind with all our might.
395 But about the false, illegitimate way,
which the people who ought to be burnt in the fire follow,
[and about] the treacherous and venal women,
the fickle and base women
(for to [these] women and their loves,
400 all is misery and sadness),

d'aqellas non devem parlar,
mas qant solament de blasmar.
Aqest iutgament, fait d'Amor,
dreitz es, c'om no·l pot far meillor.
405 E qi desdire lo volia,
ben sapchas q'eu lo·il defendria,
e·n rendria mon cavalier
si·n trobava encontra guerier.'
[L]as domnas han ben entendut,
410 e an en lur cor retengut
lo zutgament, e mes en brieu
per so qe l'oblide plus greu.
Amors lo lor ha saiellat
ab son anel d'or niellat,
415 e segnet lo de sa man destre.
Met li nom 'Paradis Terestre'.
La Cortesa d'Amor lo pren
en una caisa dousamen.
L'a mult bellament estuzat
420 el mei loec d'un samit pleiat,
e dis als barons en rient:
'Aves auszit lo zutgament
qan adreitaments an zutgat,
mas, qar sai* qe m'en sabreitz grat,
425 vos dirai* d'amor de tal loc,
don maint plor tornaran en ioc
e maint joc tornaran en plor.
Q'aital usatge han amador,
qe gai son qant be lor estai,
430 e qant han tant ni qant d'esmai,
li plaint e·il plor e·ill sospir
lur aduiszon trues q'al morir.
Mas drutz q'amor(s) vol conqistar
deu de matenent demonstrar
435 a sidonz son cor ses taïna,
s'era plus rica qe·l reïna.

fol. 35ʳ col. 1

424 MS *saz*   425 MS *diraz*

we should not speak
except only to condemn them.
This judgement, made by Love,
is just, for one cannot improve it.
405 And you know well that I would defend it
against anyone who wished to contradict it,
and would produce my knight
if I were faced with an adversary.'
   The ladies have paid careful attention,
410 and have retained the judgement
in their heart, and confided it to a document
so that they might forget it less easily.
Love has sealed it for them
with his annealed gold ring,
415 and he signs it with his right hand.
He places the name 'Earthly Paradise' on it.
The Courtliness of Love takes it
gently in a casket.
She has encased it most elegantly
420 in the middle of a folded piece of samite,
and, laughing, has said to the barons:
'You heard the judgement
when they judged prudently,
but, since I know that you will be grateful to me for it,
425 I will tell you how it sometimes goes with love,
where many tears will become a game
and many games will become tears.
For lovers have such a custom,
that they are cheerful when things are going well with them,
430 and when they have however small a trouble,
the cries and the tears and the sighs
bring them close to death.
But a lover who wants to conquer love
must immediately show
435 his lady his heart without delay,
even if she were more high-ranking than the queen.

Q'una non trobares en mil,
qe no·us en tengua per gentil,
e q'el cor no·us(is)* en sapcha grat,
440 si ben vos* fai semblant irat.
Q'il pensara: "Ges non soi laida,
pos aqest s'en vol metre en faida.
E molt faria qe felnesa,
s'aqest gentils om de mi pensa,
445 si eu non pensava de lui.
C'aisso non sap re[s] mas nos dui,*
q'el es coberts en son coratge,
q'anch no·m volg trametre messatge,
ants m'o dis totz sols de sa boca.
450 Ben conosch qe m'amors lo toca,
ben ai pus dur* cor d'un leon
s'el m'ama ez eu no voell son pron.
E molt fazia gran pecat,
s'el moria per ma beltat. *col. 2*
455 Q'el non sembla ges traïdor,
qe qan mi demonstret l'amor,
mudet tres colors en una ora:
q'el devenc pus ners d'una mora,
aqi eus devenc pus vermels
460 q'el manti* qan leva solels,
aqi eus devenc pos* blancs,
qe·l color li fugi e·l sancs."
Vec la vous, entrada en consir:
adoncs s'adobe de servir
465 lo drutz, e si plus non l'eschai.
El li soplei ab cor verai,
e digua, q'il o puosca auszir,
e fasa senblant de morir:

439 MS no^us.is. This letter cluster is very untidy in the manuscript. The *n* is malformed, a small superscript *u* (?) has been added over the back of the *o*, and a dot (indicating expunctuation of the two following letters?) comes between the first *s* and the *i*.
440 MS ñ   446 MS *dug*   451 MS *dru*   460 MS *mantz*
461 MS *pus*

For you will not find one in a thousand
who will not consider you noble,
and who in her heart will not thank you for it,
440　even if she looks angrily at you.
For she will think: "Certainly I am not ugly,
for this man is happy to suffer a rebuff [from me].
And I would be behaving very wickedly,
if this noble man were thinking of me,
445　and I were not thinking of him.
For no one else knows about this except the two of us,
since he is discreet by nature,
for he never wanted to send me a messenger,
but rather he told me all alone with his own mouth.
450　Well I know that love for me touches him,
my heart is far harder than a lion's
if he loves me and I do not want [to do that which is to] his advantage.
And I would be committing a great sin
if he died on account of my beauty.
455　For he does not seem to be a traitor at all,
for when he showed me proof of love,
he changed colour three times in an hour:
he went darker than a blackberry,
then he immediately became redder
460　than is the morning at sunrise,
then he turned white on the spot,
for his colour and his blood left him."
So there she is, absorbed in thought:
then let the lover prepare to serve,
465　even if no more than this comes his way.
Let him beseech her with a true heart,
and let him say, so that she can hear it,
and pretend to be dying:

"Domna, ben vous dei adorar
470 per la gran beltat q'en vos par.
E·l tera es santa, q'ieu o sai,
qar anc sostenc(s) vostre cors gai."
E las lacremas iescan for
per so q'el puesca emblar lo cor.
475 E giet s'als pes de genoilos,
e digua: "Dieus, reis glorios,
salva midons la gran p[ro]esa,
e la beltat q'en lei s'es mesa,
e voillatz q'el'haza merce
480 del caitiu qe ve(z) denant se. [Hand 1 finishes here.]
Dompna, Dieus e Merces mi vailla, fol. 35ᵛ col. 1
gitas me d'aqesta batailla.
Non vezes qe denant vos mor?
L'uel(s) mi volon saillir del cor,
485 tant voz hai* cellada l'amor.
Mais s'un pauch d'aqesta dolor
sentis lo vostre cors cortes,
ben sai qe mi valgra merces ...
Las! Qe hai dit? Be fas a blasmar!
490 Bella dompna, Dieus vos en guar
qe za per mi laisor color
vezas en vostre mirador.
De me non podes haver tort,
mais l'oill traïdor qe m'an mort,
495 veirament son ill traïdor:
mais aimon vos qe lor seinor.
Mais ill se raszonon vas me,
q'enquera mi fares gran be,
qe tan bel cors com m'han mostrat
500 no fo anch ses humelitat.
Dompna, aisi soi per l'asaiar.
Ab un mot mi podez ric far:
qe sol qe m'apelletz amic,
vas mi son paubre li plus ric."
505 [L]a dompna respond'a causida:
"D'una re non soi* ges marrida,

485 MS *haz*   506 MS *soz*

"My lady, well must I adore you
470 on account of the great beauty which appears in you.
And the Earth is holy, I know,
for ever having sustained your joyful self."
And tears flow forth
so that he can steal her heart.
475 And let him throw himself to his knees at her feet,
and say: "God, glorious King,
preserve in my lady the great prowess
and the beauty which is in her,
and grant that she should have mercy
480 on the miserable wretch that she sees before her.
Lady, may God and Mercy help me,
deliver me from this battle.
Do you not see that I am dying before you?
My eyes want to jump from my body,
485 so much have I hidden my love from you.
But if your courtly heart felt
a little of that sorrow,
I know full well that I would receive mercy ...
Alas! What have I said? You do well to condemn me!
490 Beautiful lady, may God protect you
from ever, on my account, seeing
a less seemly colour in your mirror.
Toward me you can do no wrong,
but the treacherous eyes which have killed me,
495 they are truly traitors:
they love you more than their lord.
But they argue with me
that you will yet do me great good,
for such a beautiful person as they have shown me
500 was never without kindness.
Lady, I am ready to be put to the test.
With one word you can make me rich:
if only you call me beloved,
compared to me the richest will be poor."
505   The lady answers amicably:
"About one thing I am not at all unhappy,

70 La Cort d'Amor

q'al mie[u] semblan, be fora mesa
en voz, si·ll cor alre no pensa, *col. 2*
l'amors de meillor q'eu non soi.*
510 Mais s'ieu so dic, no voz enoi.
Ni me perpens qe vos dirai
ab altra vez quan vos verai.
Qe vos drutz, quan vos es jauszit,
metes las dompnas en ublit.
515 E tota dompna fora druda,
si non fos per aqella cuda.
A altra vez nos veirem be:
ez el mez membre vos de me,
que·us farai de vostre plazer.
520 Que·m plaira si·m venes vezer."
Qe pro ha drutz ab domneiar
de sidons et ab gen parlar.
E qant l'a un lonc temps servit,
e·l baisa, ben l'a enriquit.
525 Qe·l menre amors qe (si) dompna fassa
a son drut, es qant vol qe i iassa*.
Qe drutz de sidonz a(ro)[i]zinatz
esdeve vilas e malvatz,
e ublida se de donar,
530 de servir e d'armas portar.
E si lo vol tener vaillent,
ab respeig lo fasa jausent.
E qant li dara so(s)* bel don,
fassa o qe·l sapcha tan bon
535 qe, qant l'aura entre sos braz,   *fol. 36ʳ col. 1*
el non cug que·l sia vertatz.
Aiso queron li drut(z) leial;
qui pus en demanda fai mal.
    [A]pres, aqest* hom convinent
540   conve q'il tenga son* cor gent
e qe se gart de fol parlar,
q'hom non puesca en lui re blasmar.

509 MS *soz*   526 MS *qe jiassa*   533 MS *so'*
539 MS *aqist*   540 MS *sos*

for it seems to me that the love of one better
than I would be well placed in you
if your heart thinks of nothing else.
510 But if I say this, may it not irritate you.
And I think that I will tell you [whether or not I will grant you what you desire]
on another occasion when I see you.
For you lovers, when you have had your pleasure,
forget ladies.
515 Indeed, every lady would be a lover
if it were not for that thought.
Another time we shall certainly see [whether I should trust you]:
within the month remember me,
and I will do something that pleases you.
520 For it would please me if you came to see me."
And it is to a lover's advantage to pay court
to his lady and to speak graciously.
And when he has served her a long time,
and she kisses him, well has she enriched him.
525 For the least love that a lady shows
to her lover, is when she wants him to sleep with her.
For when a lover has easy access to his lady
he becomes base and wicked,
and forgets to offer gifts,
530 to serve, and to carry arms.
If she wishes to keep him worthy,
let her delay making him happy.
And when she gives him her beautiful gift,
let her do it so that it is so pleasing to him
535 that when he has her in his arms,
he does not believe it to be true.
This is what loyal lovers demand;
he who asks for more does wrong.
 Afterwards, it is appropriate that this seemly
540 man should keep his heart noble
and avoid speaking foolishly,
so that one may not be able to condemn anything in him.

E d'una causa sia tricx:
s'es paubre qe se fengua ricx.
545 Q'ab un petit de bel garnir
pot hom sa paubrera cobrir.
E gard dommentre q'er iraz,
sa dompna no·l veia en la faz.
Q[e] totz hom men[tre] q'es ioios,
550 n'es trob plus bell e sa faissons.
Als messages de sa maison
serva e prometa e don
e acuella plus bellament
qe s'eron sei privat parent,
555 per so qe sa dompna la bella
auia de lui bona novella.
E haia message cortes,
mais gart qe hom non sia ges
qe miels dis dompna son talent
560 a femina qe a d'autra gent.
E fassa a cidons cembel,
manias e cordon et anel.
Qe tuit sabem ad esient
q'amistat creis per lausamet*.
565 E una causa non oblit:
ausen leis lause son marit
e digua qe molt fora pros
si non fos un petit gilos.
E s'ill s'en blasma tant ni qant,
570 cel li pot be dir aitant:
"Dousa dompna, fei q'eu dei Deu,
vos lo conoissetz miels qe eu.
Mais totz temps creirai q'el es pros
qar Dieus vol c'alte*, qu'es a voz."
575 E an soven lai on estai
e si per aventura eschai
qu'el la trob sola, mantenent
la bais e l'embras sovent.
E s'ill se suffre a forsar,
580 prenda son ioi ses demorar,

col. 2

564 MS *lausimet*   574 MS *volc alte*

In only one thing may he be sly:
if he is poor let him pretend to be rich.
545 For with a little finery
a man can disguise his poverty.
And let him mind whilst he is sad,
that his lady does not look him in the face.
For while he is joyful, every man's
550 appearance is much more handsome.
To the servants in her house
let him serve and promise and give
and [let him] welcome [them] more handsomely
than if they were close family,
555 in order that his beautiful lady
might hear good tales about him.
And let him have a courtly messenger,
but mind that it is not a man
for a lady relates her desire better
560 to a woman than to anyone else.
Let him make a lure for his lady,
sleeves, a necklace and a ring.
And we all know well and truly
that an intimate relationship grows through praise.
565 He should certainly not forget one thing:
in her hearing, to praise her husband
and to say that he would be very worthy
if he were not a little jealous.
If she complains about it, however slightly,
570 he can well say this to her:
"Sweet lady, by the faith that I owe God,
you know him better than I do.
But I will always believe that he is worthy
for God wants him to be pleasing, for he is yours."
575 And let him often go there where she is
and if, by chance, it happens
that he finds her alone, let
him at once kiss and embrace her often.
And if she allows herself to be taken by force,
580 let him take his joy without waiting,

74 LA CORT D'AMOR

qe dompna vol, per dreita escorsa,
q'hom li fasa un petit de forsa.
Q'ill no dira ia: "Fages m'o!",
mais qui la forsa, sofre so.
585 Soven deu a sidons parlar
si pot, o de loing esgardar
e mostre semblant cellador,
q'ill sapcha q'el viu de s'amor.
Enaisi deu son ioi noirir   *fol. 36ᵛ col. 1*
590 drutz, qe d'amor se vol iausir.
[L]a dompna qe vol esser druda
deu enansi esser tenguda:
con gentils om se do(mp)na soin
del sparvier qant l'a en son poin
595 qe garda qe la plu(s)ma non fraina,
deu ill gardar qe non remaina
en sa cara q'il deconveigna,
mas tota causa q'ez aveigna.
No ie meta causa qe i nosa,
600 mais be pot gitar aigua rosa
qe qui la baisza per gran dousor
cug q'haia·l cors plen de flor.
De si meteissa sia gilosa,
tant vol esser coinda e ginnosa,
605 qe tota dompna es bella e cara
qe se ten cointament et esgara.
E es de tot en tot perduda
si car e gent non es tenguda
e loing sapch'om retener grat
610 d'aco q'il aura esgardat.
Ab vertat e ses tricaria,
demostre* bella conpainia
e ill paresca sotz la gimpla
gai[a] re e corteisa et simpla.
615 E qui ven a leis corteiar   *col. 2*
sapcha gen respondr'e parlar,
e gart per plana gentilesa
qe non diga mot de malesa,

612 MS *demostro*

for a lady desires, for correct appearance,
that a man compel her a little.
For she will never say: "Do it to me!",
but if a man forces her, she allows it.
585 He must speak to his lady often
if he can, or watch her from a distance
and show himself to be discreet,
so that she may know that he lives for love of her.
Thus must the lover who wishes to
590 enjoy love nurture his joy.
    The lady who desires to be beloved
   must be groomed thus:
just as the noble man takes care
of the sparrow hawk when he has it on his fist
595 and minds that he does not break its plumage,
she must mind that there does not remain
anything on her face which is unseemly,
but everything that is appropriate.
Let her not apply anything that would harm it,
600 but well may she sprinkle it with rose water
so that whoever kisses her out of sheer sweetness
thinks that her body is full of flowers.
Let her be jealous of herself,
so much does she want to be gracious and refined,
605 for every lady is beautiful and beloved
who behaves graciously and pays attention to herself.
And she is entirely lost
if she is not richly and nobly groomed
and long may a man be able to be grateful
610 that she has looked at him.
Truly and without deception,
let her give proof of fine company
and under her head-dress may she appear
a gay, courtly and unaffected creature.
615 To whoever comes to court her
may she certainly know how to respond and speak,
and may she mind through sheer nobility
that she may not speak an uncouth word,

ni de folia ni d'orguell.
620 Qui gent parla semena e cuell,
q'el semena ensenha(i)ment
e cuell laus e prez de la gent.
E gar·s q'il mot sian causit
per so qe meills sion graszit,
625 ab vertat e ses tricaria;
si corr[an]* con sen e coindia,
qe gen parlars creis son seinor(s)
si con [lo] ros acreis (e) la flor(s);*
per qe dompna gen enparlada
630 sera totz temps pros e onrada.
E sapcha tan gen acuillir
qe qant venra al departir,
qar sol auran ab leis parlat,
cuidon li fol esser senat.
635 E·l savi digan: "Dousa res,
mult es vostre cors de ioi ples,
molt sabes mesclar cointamen
corteszi'a foudat ab sen,
ez urguell ab humilitat.
640 Ancheis hauri'hom fait privat
un roissinol, c'om vos auies
far ni dir qe·us desconvenies.
Vostre dit han aitan d'onor, *fol. 37ʳ col. 1*
l'un son bon e l'autre meillor."
645 Son amic non trich [j]a ges,
ni·l digua mais so qe vers es.
Que dompna e polpra e samit
trobares alques d'un aqit,
qe la porpra, pois es solada,
650 non pot esser iamais gensada,
on plus la non laisezes;
et dompna, puis engans i es,
ni pot esser d'engan represa,
jamais non pot esser cortesa
655 ni, pus c'om pot estain d[a]urar,
non pot iamais son prez cobrar.

626 MS *cors*   628 MS *si conrasa creis elaflors*

nor a foolish or a proud one.
620 Whoever speaks nobly sows and reaps,
for he sows good instruction
and reaps praise and esteem from [other] people.
Let her mind that her words be well chosen
so that they may be the better received,
625 truthfully and honestly;
let them flow sensibly and charmingly,
for noble speech makes its lord grow
just as the dew makes a flower grow;
which is why a well-spoken lady
630 will always be worthy and honoured.
Indeed, may she know how to receive people so nobly
that when it comes to parting,
purely because they have spoken to her,
the foolish believe they are wise.
635 Let the wise men say: "Sweet creature,
your person is most full of joy,
you can most gracefully and judiciously
combine courtliness and folly,
and pride with humility.
640 Sooner would a man have tamed
a nightingale, than hear about you
doing or saying anything unseemly.
Your words have so much honour,
some are good, the others better."
645 She should not deceive her companion at all,
nor should she tell him anything but the truth.
For a lady and purple cloth and samite
you will find somewhat similar,
for the purple cloth, once it is dirty,
650 can never be cleaned again,
however much you were to avoid soiling it further;
likewise a lady, once deception is in her,
and she can be blamed for deceitfulness,
can never be courteous
655 nor, any more than one can gild tin,
can she ever recover her reputation again.

E ill cabeill ssion coindament
estretz ab fil d'aur o(n) d'argent.
Una sotilleta garlanda
660 gart q'uns pel front no s'en espanda*,
e sion per plan agardat
e volt de polpra o de cendat
mais un sol petit c'om en veia,
qe·l mons digua de fina enveia:
665 "Ben ha(n) l'onor e la proesa,
dompna, del mon, qi vos adesa".
E anon dreit e per un fil
e coindament sion sotil
li sobrecil sotz lo bel front;
670 lo mentonet bel e rodont; *col. 2*
las dents paucas e menudetas;
bel nas e bocas vermelletas,
ben faitas ad obs de baisar
cui Deus volria tan onrar;
675 blanc col; e porte sas bellas mans
en gans, qe no·ls veza vilans;
bella borsa, bella centura,
com s'era tot fait en peintura,
e paresca bella e dolgada*
680 sotz la bella boc[l]a daurada.
D'una re se deu donar cura:
com l'estei be sa vestidura,
gent vestent* e gent afublans,
amorosa en totz* sos semblas.
685 Bel sion li vestit defors,
la camisa qe toca·l cors
sia bella, sotilss e blanca
co·l neus en uvern sor la branca.
Gent se cals e gent port sos pes
690 e an ab dompnas de gran pres.
Am gentils omes, qi qe·n gronda,
parle gent et digua e responda.
La gimpla non sia ges mesa
el cap a gisa de pagesa,

660 MS *espenda*   679 MS *dolguda*   683 MS *vistent*   684 MS *tota*

Let her hair be charmingly
tied with a thread of gold or silver.
Let an exquisitely delicate garland
660   prevent a hair from dangling down across her brow,
and let it [her hair] appear smooth
and be twisted with purple cloth or silk
just a little so that one may see it,
so that all may say out of pure envy:
665   "Anyone who is in contact with you,
lady, has the best honour and merit of the world".
Let her eyebrows run straight and like a thread
and be gracefully delicate
below her beautiful brow;
670   [let] her chin [be] beautiful and round;
her teeth small and tiny;
[she should have] a beautiful nose and rosy red lips,
well made for kissing
whomever God may wish to honour so greatly;
675   [let her have] a white neck; and let her wear gloves on her
beautiful hands, so that no churl may see them;
[she should have] a beautiful purse and a fine belt,
as if it were all done in a painting,
and may she appear beautiful and slender
680   below the beautiful gilt buckle.
She must concern herself with one thing:
that her clothing should suit her well,
that she should be finely and elegantly dressed
and cloaked, agreeable in all her ways.
685   Let her outer clothing be beautiful,
let the blouse which touches her body
be beautiful, delicate and white
like the snow on the branch in winter.
Let her shoes be elegant and let her tread gracefully
690   and accompany ladies of great merit.
With gentlemen, whoever may scold her for this,
let her speak nobly and converse and reply.
Let her head-dress not be at all placed
on her head in the manner of a peasant woman,

80 *La Cort d'Amor*

695 an[s] sia coindament pausada
sobre las bellas crins planada.
E si deu anar en coasa, *fol. 37ᵛ col. 1*
d'un cordonet daurat la fasa,
que l'aur[i]pel e li boton
700 rescemblon tuit d'una faison.
Gent si tengua, sovent se bain
e ab nedesa se* compain,
ves tot lo mont cuberta e cellada,
mais son amic sia aizinada
705 quant sera luecs ni d'avinent.
Eu hai* ben dig al parlament
so qe li bon drut tenran car
e fara·l gilos enrabchar.'
[C]ortesia ditz: 'Dompn[a] pros,
710 d'aiso m'acort eu ben ab vos,
qe molt es gilos en gran pena.
Qe s'el bat sa moiller, forsena;
adoncs pens'ella: "Ar amarai,
pois atrestant de blasme(t) i hai!";
715 e puis c'ave tot en [un] trait
qe dis: "Mals es ma part e fait!",
e el la baisa e la percola,
adons la destrui e l'afola,
q'ella pensa: "Molt m'aima fort.
720 Ben sufriria dreig e tort".
Per nient seri'on gellos:
batre ni blandir n'es ges* bos;
mais lais lor on anar sospe*,
e venia lur, bona merce *col. 2*
725 Amors, aiso qe·ls ven a grat.'
E ha devant se esgardat*
e vi Merce venir corrent
qe volg esser el parlament.
E qan l'an vista li baron,
730 no i a cel non sapcha hom.

702 MS *so*   706 MS *haz*   722 MS *ñg es*
723 MS *lospe*   726 MS *esgardit*

695 but let it be gracefully rested
on her beautiful smoothed locks.
If she should wear her hair in a plait,
let her fix it in place with a gilt thread,
and let her garment and buttons
700 match each other exactly.
Let her keep herself delightful and bathe often
and keep company with cleanliness,
subtle and discreet toward everyone,
but accommodating toward her companion
705 when it is meet and proper.
Well have I told the assembly
what the good lovers will hold dear
and will enrage the jealous man.'
   Courtliness says: 'Worthy lady,
710 for my part I agree with you very much about this,
that the jealous man is in great distress.
For if he beats his wife, he is out of his mind;
then she thinks: "Now I *will* love,
as I have just the same blame for it!";
715 and it so happens at the same time
that he says: "Misfortune is my lot indeed!",
and he kisses her and embraces her,
then harms her and ill-treats her,
so that she thinks: "He loves me very much.
720 He would be prepared to put up with anything".
There is no point in a man being jealous:
beating and flattery are never any good;
but let a man abandon suspicion of them [noble lovers],
and let that which pleases them
725 come to them by the kind grace of Love.'
And she [Courtliness] has looked ahead
and seen Mercy arriving in haste
for he wanted to be in the assembly.
And when the barons have seen him,
730 there is not one who does not know the man well.

Mont polsa son caval lo flancs,
per un pauc qe non es [e]stancs.
Aqest trameto l'amador,
per faire clam a Fin'Amor
735 de las dompnas descominals.
Molt cuitas (c)a tost le vasals,
a tant es a cort desendutz;
tuit diçon: 'Ben siaz vengutz!',
e el respon: 'E Deu[s] sal vos,
740 Amors, e to_ts_* vostre[s] baros,
e confonda aqu(i)els qes eu vei:
la Cobezesa ez Orguei,
q'entro c'aici m'an encausat.
A qant loncs temps m'an trabaillat!
745 Amors, tot lo mont han delit,
dompnas vos an mes en oblit.
Qe c'era fils d'emperador,
s'es paupre, gens non a d'amor,
mais aqell es onratz ses failla
750 qe promet los diniers e·l bailla.
E qant ha lors diniers pagat,
e·l fausa los ha es_t_uchat*,
il dis: "Enqer non es sasons:
autra ves trametrem per vos".
755 El ten l'e aquella balansa
e confont la bona esperansa.
E qant non ha plus qe donar,
il lo gaba e laissa l'estar,
l'orgoilosza, cui Deus abata
760 cant vei lo mantel d'escarlata
e lo var e lo cenbelin,
la pols qe mena lo traïn!
La filla d'un villan caitiu
vos fara de mil drutz esqiu.
765 E Amors deu esse[r] umils,
on plus es rica, e plus gentils.
E s'er filla d'un cavaler
e negus autr_e_* om l'enqer,

fol. 38ʳ col. 1

740 MS *tost*   752 MS *escuchat*   768 MS *autra*

He hits his horse's flanks hard
so that it is almost dead with exhaustion.
Lovers are sending him
to petition True Love
735 about severe ladies.
The man came galloping up at top speed,
then he dismounted at the court;
all say: 'You are welcome!',
and he replies: 'God save you,
740 Love, and all your barons,
and confound those that I see:
Covetousness and Pride
who have pursued me right up to here.
What a long time they have bothered me!
745 Love, they have undone the whole world:
ladies have forgotten you.
For [a man], even if he were an emperor's son,
if he is poor, has nothing from love whatsoever,
but he who promises money and power
750 is honoured without fail.
When he has then paid her the money,
and the false woman has pocketed it,
she says: "It is not yet the right time:
we will send for you on another occasion".
755 And she holds him in that uncertainty
and confounds good hope.
Then, when he has nothing else to give,
she mocks him and leaves him standing,
the proud woman, God confound her
760 when I see the scarlet coat
and the vair and the sable,
and the dust that the train shifts!
The daughter of a base wretch
will make you lose a thousand lovers.
765 Love certainly ought to be kind and more gracious
where she [the lady] has higher rank [than her lover].
And if she is a knight's daughter
whom no other man is wooing,

ela dira: "Ges no·m eschai,
770 ne ia vilan non amarai".
E fai pecat s'enaisi i clama,
qe totz om val lo rei qe ama.
Aici·m trameton l'amador
qe vos regardetz lur dolor.
775 Per vos son mort et enganatz,
de lor avetz torts e pecatz,
e fares mal vostra fasenda
si de vos non han bella esmenda; *col. 2*
e c'om digua q'a bon signor
780 han servit, membre·us de lor.'
[S]o dis Amors: 'La[s] dompnas son
tota·ls plus dousa[s] res del mon.
Eu soi lur et ellas son mias;
e be conois qe lur follias
785 lor tolon garen de lur pron,
qe quant om dis: "A vos me don,
bella dousa res, ses engan;
a Dieu et a(b) vos mi coman;
dompna, vezas ma bona fe,
790 si no·m retenes, morai me.
Caitiu, q'hai dit? Dompna, no·us pes
qe·l grans deszirers qe·m ten pres
me fai lo maltrait descobrir.
E si vos mi fazes morir
795 mi plaz, mas no i haures honor
s'auciez vostre servidor.
Q'eu sai be qe per vos servir
nasqiei e quant li dous sospir
me coiton tan qe per vos plor,
800 beu las lagremas de dousor
e dic: 'Oillz, bona feses anc nat
(qar haves per midonz plorat)
qe·n val mens'", s'ella·l respont gent
e ce merceira coindament,
805 e dis: "Amicx, eu vos sai grat *fol. 38ᵛ col. 1*
de ço⁕ qe m'avetz presentat.

806 MS *co*

she will say: "This is by no means fitting for me,
770 nor will I ever love any uncouth man".
And she commits a sin if she thus complains about it,
for every man who loves is worth a king.
The lovers send me here
in order that you consider their pain.
775 Through you they are killed and deceived,
concerning them you are wrong and sinful,
and you do your duty poorly
if they do not have a fine recompense from you;
and so that one may say that they have served
780 a good lord, remember them.'
    Love says this: 'Ladies are
all the sweetest creatures in the world.
I am theirs and they are mine;
and well I know that their follies
785 deprive them of a guarantee of their advantage,
for when a man says: "I give myself to you,
beautiful and sweet creature, without deceit;
to God and to you I commend myself;
lady, see my good faith,
790 if you do not stop me, I will die.
Miserable wretch! What have I said? Lady, do not let it weigh
    upon you
that the great desire which captivates me
makes me disclose how badly you have treated me.
And if you cause me to die
795 it will please me, but you will have no honour from it
if you kill your servant.
For well I know that I was born in order to
serve you, and when the sweet sighs
torment me so much that I cry on your account,
800 I drink the tears of sweetness
and say: 'Eyes, fortunately you never did anything
(for you have cried on account of my lady)
which makes me worth less'", then she replies nobly
and graciously has mercy on him,
805 and says: "My friend, I am grateful to you
for that which you have offered me.

Eu voell qe per me siaz pros,
e vos tenrai gai e ioios",
ez haurai son pres retengut,
810 e l'autra aura fait coinde drut,
e pueis s'il en conois s'onor,
pot en faire son amador.
Merces, aitant farai per vos:
qe do[m]pnas metran orguel jos,
815 mais amara·l plus orguilosa
son drut q'ar cel cui [es] esposa,
e li drut seran lur senior.
E portas lur aqesta flor*
per entresenia q'ieu lur man
820 q'ill auran tot so q'ill voran.
Las cobezesas, don vos clamaz,
jamais non vos entremetaz,
Corteszia las a'tzinadas,
aquellas qi qeron soldadas,
825 er getat de ma compania.
Non voell c'om lur son en la via,
qe dompna qe diniers demanda
es traïtris e mercaanda,
e non saubon tant de raubar
830 li galiot de sobre mar.
E s'ela me fai* mon plazer
als diners en dei grat saber. *col. 2*
A leis non dei portar onor
segond lo jutguament d'Amor.'
835 [A]mors levet del parlament
e tuit li baron eissament.
La Cortesa d'Amor lo sona:
'Seiner, qar non portes corona,
qe reis es de trastota gent
840 apres Christus l'omnipotent?'
La corona l'han aportat,
Jois l'a mantenent coronat.

818–31 The MS lesson is very faint and smudged here.   831 MS *faz*

I desire that through me you may be worthy,
and I will keep you gay and joyful",
and I will have preserved his worth
810 and she will have made him a charming lover,
and if she then recognizes his honour,
she can make him her partner.
Mercy, this I will do through you:
that ladies will cast down pride,
815 and the proudest lady will love her lover
more than she now does the man whose wife she is,
and the lovers will be their lords.
Take them this flower
as a sign that I command them
820 to have all that they want.
Never again concern yourself with
the covetous women of whom you complain,
Courtliness has dealt with them,
those who seek payment,
825 [and] now [they are] banished from my company.
I do not want anyone to speak to them on the street,
for a lady who requests money
is a traitor and a merchant,
and pirates on the high seas
830 do not know as much about robbing [as she does].
If she fulfils my pleasure
I must be grateful to the money.
To her I should not bring honour
according to the judgement of Love.'
835   Love stood up from the assembly
   as did all the barons together.
The Courtliness of Love addresses [him] as follows:
'My lord, why do you not wear a crown,
you who are king of all people
840 after Christ the All-Powerful?'
They have brought him a crown,
and Joy has crowned him at once.

88 La Cort d'Amor

      La fontaina pres a bruiz,
      e la conca a reten[t]ir,
845 c'om no sap negun* estrument
      el mo qe* s'acordes tan gent.
      L'arbre l'encoron a sopleiar
      qe l'avia vist coronar.
      Del prat li sailon per lo vis,
850 violetas et flor[s] de lis,
      e en tot lo mon non a flor
      no·l fasa tant qant pod d'onor.
      Qant venc al intrar del castel,
      comenson a cantar li aucel,
855 e·l Foc d'Amor ad abrasar,
      e las donzellas a dansar;
      e l'amador canton dous lais.
      Tan rica cort no er'iamais!
      Pels deis si asezon matenent,   *fol. 39ʳ col. 1*
860 las flors els ausels mesclament;
      el mon no es volta ni lais
      l'ausel non canto en palais.
      Del maniar ia no er parlat,
      c'om no sap poison ni dintat
865 qe a cors d'ome fasa ben
      no i aia tan quan i coven.
      Qant son asis, la guaita cria:
      'Cobezesa es morta e aunida,
      e havem Orguel abatut.
870 Ara si guardon li cornut,
      qe mon[s] senior[s] porta corona.
      A(l)quil han* ioi, cui el en dona,
      e totz om es malaüros
      que non s'acompaina ab vos.
875 Nos havem fag lo iugament
      d'Amor, fols es qui non l'aprent.'
      Amors comencet a seinnar,
      e anceis que volges maniar
      el dis: 'Senior Deu glorios,
880 tot aquest ioi teng eu de vos.

      845 MS *sat negus*   846 MS *qa*   872 MS *alquel han*

The fountain started to sound,
and the shell to resonate,
845 such that no man knows any instrument
in the world which was so pleasantly harmonious.
The trees which saw him crowned
press in on him in order to bow down.
From the meadow, violets and lilies
850 throw themselves into his sight,
and in all the world there is no flower
which does not do what it can to honour him.
When he came to the entrance of the castle,
the birds begin to sing,
855 and the Fire of Love to blaze,
and the young ladies to dance;
and the lovers sing sweet lays.
There never was such a splendid court!
At once the flowers sit down all together
860 amongst the birds around the table;
there is no song nor lay in the world
that the birds do not sing in the palace.
The food will never be spoken of,
for one knows of no beverage or delicacy
865 which is beneficial to the human constitution
which is not there in suitable amounts.
Once they are seated, the watchman cries:
'Covetousness is dead and dishonoured,
and we have cast down Pride.
870 Now the cuckolds beware
for my lord wears a crown.
They have joy, those to whom he gives it,
and every man is unfortunate
who does not keep company with you.
875 We have made the judgement
of Love, foolish is he who does not learn it.'
Love started to make the sign of the cross,
and before he wanted to eat
he said: 'Glorious Lord God,
880 I hold all this joy from you.

Seiner, la[u] vostra gran merces
de l'onor qu'ieu hai e del[s] bes.'
[Q]uant han le[s] premiers mes aiutz,
Ris e Deport[z] i es vengutz
885 (Joglar foron a Fin'Amor)
ab Na Coindia, sa seror, *col. 2*
qui vai per sol molt coindament,
dansan ab un cimblos d'argent.
Tan gai son qe lor cor lur vola.
890 L'us ag arpa, l'autre viola.
Per las taulas viras los drutz,
de la gran dousor esperdutz.
Las donzellas cuion sautar
fors de las taulas per dansar,
895 mais Amors o ha conogut,
q'ha por Rire son cap mogut.
Pel seneschal lur a mandat
qe·l ioglar sion escoutat
q'el vol pueis, a tot lur plaszer,
900 se deporton a lur voler,
e fe qu'il devon, non lur pes,
q'a(m)l soffrir vez'om li cortes.
[L]i ioglar se proschon del rei
. . . .
Rire parlet enantz Deport:
905 'Amors, molt vos fan estrain tort
li lausengier(s) de lin Iutas.
Cui mal[s] fuecs las lengas* abras,
qe li phylosof e·l doctor
jutguon lausengier(s) per traïdor.
910 Sia breus sa raszon ou longa
lo tot o·l plus sera mensonga.
Ai Dieus! Con lait han desconfit
con han dompnas e drutz partit. *fol. 39ᵛ col. 1*
Qe·l drutz dis: "Dousa res causida,
915 mout vos avia ben servida;
totz mos avers e mos tesors
era lo vostre gentil cors.

907 MS *lenguas*. There are two small expunctuation dots below the *u*.

Lord, I praise your great mercy
for the honour and the good things I have.'
   When they had had the first courses,
   Laughter and Distraction arrived
885 (they were jongleurs to True Love)
with Lady Grace, his sister,
who glides gracefully,
dancing with a silver cymbal.
They are so merry that she steals their hearts.
890 One had a harp, the other a viol.
Amongst the tables you would see the lovers,
giddy from the great sweetness.
The maidens intend to jump
away from the tables in order to dance,
895 but Love, who has made a gesture of his head
in favour of Laughter, has spotted this.
Through the seneschal he ordered them
that the jongleurs should be heard
for he wishes, for their pleasure,
900 that they sport as they wish afterwards,
and by the faith that they owe, that they should not mind,
for one recognizes courtly men in [their] patience.
   The jongleurs approach the king
   . . . .
Laughter spoke before Distraction:
905 'Love, the slanderers of Judas' descent
do you a very cruel wrong.
Let an evil fire burn their tongues,
for the philosophers and the doctors
condemn the slanderer as a traitor.
910 Whether his [a slanderer's] discourse be short or long,
all or most [of it] will be a lie.
Ah God! How horribly they have destroyed [love]
when they have divided ladies and lovers.
For the lover says: "Sweet, amiable creature,
915 I used to serve you very well;
your noble person was
all my possession and my treasure.

92   La Cort d'Amor

          Er non seretz iamai laidida
          e doncs, dompna, qe·m val ma vida?
920   Ben m'er dura res, ez amara(i)
          se lla vostra convinens cara,
          qe fai tot lo mon resplandir,
          se laissa qe vas me no·s vir.
          Faita an li lauzeiador
925   com aqel qe damnia* la flor
          del vergier qe vol sordeiar,
          qe non puesca pois frug far.
          Zois era floritz antre nos,
          mais lausengier(s) l'en han secos
930   qe no i han laissat flor ni foilla,
          per qe l'aigua del cor mi moilla
          mos oills; mas cant a trop tengut
          lais temps, e qe za fort* plogut,
          plaz mais lo soleals, e·l bels iorns
935   ez es a tota gens sozorns.
          Atressi creis e dobla zais
          apres lo maltraig, e val mais,
          per q'eu, dompna, no·m desesper,
          ni ia Dieus no m'en don lezer
940   qe de vos s·parton mei deszir,   *col. 2*
          nes lo zorn qe volrai morir.
          Qe qan per aventura ven
          q'eu dorm ez estau tan ben,
          dompna, q'adonc soi* eu ab vos,
945   e remir las vostras faisos,
          e cug ades ab vos parlar
          privadamens, si com soil far,
          e cug q'ades siatz enblada
          de la cambra en qe es gardada,
950   lo grans zoi[s] me fai ricedar;
          e quant eu non vos puosc trobar
          tan granda dolor emdeven
          q'ieu me mervell qar non forsen.
          E Dieus! Qe me pod conortar?
955   Qan mi soven del embrasar

925 MS *danmia*   933 MS *feit*   944 MS *soz*

Now you will never be insulted,
but so, lady, what use is my life?
920 It will certainly be a hard and bitter thing for me
if your seemly face,
which makes the whole world resplendent,
stops turning toward me.
The slanderers have done this
925 like him who damages the flower
in the orchard that he wants to ruin
so that it may not bear fruit.
Joy had bloomed between us,
but slanderers have stripped it
930 so that they have left not a flower or leaf of it,
which is why the water of my heart dampens
my eyes; but when bad weather has lasted
too long and it has certainly rained hard,
the sun and a fine day are [all the] more pleasing
935 and are a respite for everyone.
Similarly, joy grows and doubles
after pain, and is worth more,
which is why I do not despair, lady,
nor may God ever allow the possibility
940 of my desires abandoning you,
not even the day I am about to die.
For when, by chance, it happens
that I sleep and rest so well,
lady, that I am with you
945 and I gaze upon your face,
and straight away think I am speaking to you
privately, as I am used to doing,
and immediately I think that you have been taken away
from the room in which you are guarded,
950 the great joy makes me grow wealthy;
but when I cannot find you
such a great sadness occurs
that I am astounded that I don't go mad.
Ah God! What can comfort me?
955 When I remember the embrace

94   LA CORT D'AMOR

    e del do͟us* baiszar e del rire,
    Amiga, ben deuria ausire.
    Qe vos estaz, ma dousa amiga,
    aisi com la ro͟za* ab ortiga,
960 qe vos es dousa e plazens
    ez es pauzada entr'avols gens."
    Enaisi plaing lo drutz e·l druda
    es mil aitans morta e venduda,
    q'el non ausa ab omen parlar,
965 ni gen vestir ni gen causar,
    ne s'ausa deportar ni rire,
    qe non haia paor d'aucire.   *fol. 40ʳ col. 1*
    Ez esta en gran penssamen,
    e ditz en son cor mout soven:
970 "Bels amics, haurai iamai aisze
    qe vos percolle ni vos baisze?
    Eu non. Faillit son mei* deport;
    me e vos han lauzengier(s) mort."
    Amors, penren en ia veniansa
975 ni·n portarem escut ni lansa
    sobre·ls lausengiers traïdors
    qe tolon las dousas amors.'
    Plasers, lo senescals d'Amor,
    parlet en luoc de son seinor.
980 Molt fo pros e cortes e vi(a)stes,
    e savis hom e bon legistes.
    [E] ha li dit: 'Bels amics bos,
    gent aves dig vostras razos,
    mais tot quant aves devizat,
985 ha hoi Cortezia iugat.
    Q'ill ditz q'ab sen et ab mesura
    pot hom aver amor segura,
    e si lausengier son Marcos,
    hom lur deu esser Salamos.
990 Ja no er qe gilos non sia,
    mais ieu dic qe re non enbria,

956 MS *dōs*   959 MS *raza*   972 MS *mez*

and the sweet kissing and the laughter,
my love, it should well kill me.
For you are, my sweet love,
like the rose with the nettle,
960 for you are sweet and pleasing
and you are placed among base people."
The lover laments thus and his beloved
is dead and betrayed a thousand times as much
for she does not dare to speak to a man,
965 or to dress nobly or to speak nobly;
nor does she dare to amuse herself or laugh,
without being afraid of being killed.
And she is greatly preoccupied,
and she frequently says in her heart:
970 "Handsome companion, shall I never have the
opportunity to embrace or kiss you?
Not I. My delights have stopped;
the slanderers have killed me and you."
Love, we shall certainly take our revenge for this
975 and on this account will carry a shield and a lance
against the treacherous slanderers
who put a stop to sweet love affairs.'
Pleasure, the seneschal of Love,
spoke in stead of his lord.
980 He was worthy and courtly and lively,
a wise man and a good lawyer.
    And he said to him: 'Fine good friend,
    nobly have you presented your case,
but all of what you have related,
985 Courtliness has judged today.
For she says that with judgement and moderation
one can have a secure love,
and if slanderers are Marcos,
one must be Solomon to them.
990 It will never come about that there are no slanderers,
but I say that it does not matter at all,

96 *La Cort d'Amor*

      qe mos seihner es poderos,
      qe ia l[a]uszengiers ni gelos
      no cera·n dan a drut cortes,   *col. 2*
995 ans lur pro mas be lur pes,
      qar en luoc fan tan gran paor,
      q'el non parlara auien lor.
      E si con l'aurs el f(l)uec s'escura,
      aqes(i)ta paor los meillura,
1000 q'el si gara de fol parlar
      e fai ab sen tot son afar.
      E s'il van si don'espian,
      ill fai* vezer lur bel semblan.
      Ab tal don gaire* no li cal
1005 a qe cobre son ioi coral.'
      [A]pres ditz Deportz: 'Gran faillida
      fai aqel qe sidonz oblida,
      qan de son gent cors [es] onrat.
      El non l'a trait ni galiat,
1010 antz l'a tengut gai e iausen,
      fait [li] tan enveios prezen,
      coves de son bell acuillir,
      e l'a volgut tan enreqir
      qe si ag maltrait de s'amor,
1015 ar lo i ha tornat en dousor
      e donat de sas bellas res,
      mangas, cordos et orfres,
      e si li mostra puei cor truan,
      no se pot desfendre d'engan,
1020 antz contrafai lo traïdor
      qu'es rics de l'aver son seinhor,   *fol. 40^v col. 1*
      e pueis met contra luei l'aver,
      e·s pena de lui decaçer.
      Ges non deu haver cor volatge,
1025 antz deu tener ferm coratge,
      qe bona dompna non peiiura,
      antz enancha ades e meillura.
      Q'eu prez mais la valor e·l sen
      de dompna non fai* lo ioven,

1003 MS *faz*   1004 MS *gaere*   1029 MS *faz*

for my lord is powerful,
so a slanderer or a jealous man
will never pose a threat to the courtly lover,
995 but rather their [the slanderers'] advantage is much more detrimental to themselves,
for sometimes they cause such great fear
that he will not speak in their hearing.
And just as gold purifies itself in the fire,
this fear improves him,
1000 for he will avoid speaking foolishly
and conduct his affair entirely with judgement.
If they come spying on his lady,
she lets them see a beautiful expression.
With such a gift she cares not
1005 from whom she hides her sincere joy.'
   Then Distraction says: 'He who
neglects his lady commits a great fault
when he is honoured by her noble person.
She did not betray or deceive him,
1010 on the contrary she kept him gay and joyful,
gave him such a desirable gift,
the promise of her fine welcome,
and wanted to enrich him so much
that if he had pain from his love,
1015 she has now turned it into sweetness for him
and given him sleeves, necklaces and
braids from her beautiful possessions,
and if he then shows her a base heart
she cannot defend herself from deceit,
1020 but rather, he imitates the traitor
who is rich from his lord's possessions
and then uses the wealth against him
and strives to ruin him.
He must certainly not have a fickle heart,
1025 but rather keep his heart constant,
for a good lady does not get worse,
but rather constantly advances and improves.
For I rate the valour and the judgement
of a lady higher than I do the youth,

1030 e si com frugs val mais qe flor,
val mais qe beltat la valor.
Mais cant es bona la canchos,
la laissa·l ioglar enoios;
aital fai qe tota sazon
1035 non fai si donz qe·l sapcha bon,
e si fai apres autr'amia,
ni autra qi, ço sapchatz*, s'i fia
e ll'apella son amador
. . . .
qe totz temps es de ioi deiuna
1040 la boca qez enqier mas una.'
'[S]i m'aiut Dieus!' (so dis Coindia),
'Ben fai mal qe sidonz oblia,
e mal fai dompna qe delonza
son amic pois per lui es coin[j]a.
1045 Qe ia non sera tan zinnosa,
daus pueis qe si fai vergoinosa
d'aqel qe volria aver pres,
non faza lo vilan cortes.
E percaz son ben e s'onor,
1050 q'enantz qe li lauzeniador
o haion saubut ni sentit,
deuria·n haver son ioi complit.
Qar tost passon li mercadier
lo pas on tornan li stradier,
1055 e qan ill son en via segura,
ill van bellamen l'enblaüra.
Atressi dompna non deu a len
penre son ioi, mas torne·s(on) gen
e deu gardar qe fin'amors gaia
1060 per lonc enplaidar non dechaia.
E nos deporton nos oimais,
e·ll auzell movan tut lur lais,
e veian si s'acordon gen
l'auzell e nostri estrumen.
1065 Qi apres aisso au las voz
e·l ioi qe menon entre·ls totz,
ben ha pus dur lo cor d'aziman'*

1037 MS cosapchatz   1067 MS oziman

col. 2

1030 and just as the fruit is worth more than the flower,
merit is worth more than beauty.
But when the song is good,
the tiresome jongleur stops singing it;
he behaves such that the whole time
1035 he does not do for his lady what pleases her,
and then he gets another partner,
and the other woman who, know this, trusts in him
and calls him her lover
. . . .
for the mouth that requires more than one
1040 is always starved of joy.'
'God help me!' (thus spoke Grace),
'He who neglects his lady commits a great wrong
and a lady does wrong who rebuffs
her lover after she has been amiable on his account.
1045 For once she acts ashamed
of the one she would have liked to have taken,
she will never be so cunning
as to make the uncouth man courtly.
But let her pursue her advantage and her honour,
1050 so that before the slanderers
have known or have learnt it,
she has accomplished her joy.
For merchants travel quickly on
the path where highwaymen circulate,
1055 and when they are on a safe road
they stroll along calmly.
In the same way, a lady must not slowly
take her joy, but let her graciously return [to her lover]
and she must mind that gay true love
1060 may not decline on account of long beseeching.
And let us henceforth make merry,
and let the birds begin all their lays,
and let the birds and our instruments
see if they can combine harmoniously.
1065 Whoever then hears the voices
and the joy that they produce between them all,
he has a heart much harder than a diamond'

.... [*A blank line is left in the MS here.*]
[H]onors e Valors e·l Baillessa
d'Amor, qe re mas ioi non pessa,
1070 son vengudas ad auzir lo(s) chan.
E son vestudas d'un semblan,
d'un blanc samit ab floretas
d'aur; capelz han de violetas.
Qant ellas entron el palais, *fol. 41ʳ col. 1*
1075 sapchatz qe·l cortz en val ja mais.
La Baillessa d'Amor a presa
Honor; deiost'Amor l'a mesa.
El ac gran ioi qan l'ag veszuda:
vas si la streing, baisar la cuda,
1080 mas sas gen[s] lo feiron suffrir
per paor q'en fezes murir
de plan'envia, dos o tres,
qe la dompna es tan bella res.
E ditz: 'Dompna, ben foz onrada
1085 ma bocca, si·us hages baisada,
q'ieu non soi dignes, dous'amiga,
....
Qe tan ha d'onor vostra boca
qe tot es sans qant a leis toca.
Vos mi tenes en tal liam,
1090 con pus m'aucises, no m'en clam.
Per q'auciretz vos, dompna bella,
celui qi vas vos no·s revella?
Vostra dousa amors m'esperona.
Pos bella es, siatz me bona
1095 e non fassatz l'auszellador
q'apella e trai ab dousor
l'auszel tro qe l'a en sa tela,
pueis l'auci e·l destrui e·l pela.
Dompna, l'uell, pus luszent q'estela,
1100 regardon, pus son cor no·us cela,
le vostre sers qe tant vos ama. *col. 2*
Per Dieu e per vos se reclama.
Per mil vez siatz ben venguda!
Gran[s] joia m'es al cor creguda

. . . .
    Honour and Merit and the Bailiff
of Love, who thinks nothing but joy,
1070 have come to hear the singing.
They are all dressed the same
in white silk embroidered with small flowers
of gold; they have crowns of violets.
When they enter into the palace,
1075 know that the court is surely worth more as a result.
The Bailiff of Love has taken
Honour and placed her next to Love.
He felt great joy when he saw her:
he clasps her to him, and intends to kiss her,
1080 but his people made him be patient
for fear that he might kill,
through sheer envy, two or three people,
for the lady is such a beautiful creature.
He says: 'Lady, greatly honoured would my
1085 mouth have been, if I had kissed you,
as I am not worthy, sweet companion,
. . . .
For your mouth has so much honour
that everything which touches it is holy.
You hold me on such a tether
1090 that however much you kill me, I do not complain.
Why, beautiful lady, are you killing
the man who does not revolt against you?
Your sweet love provokes me.
As you are beautiful, may you be kind to me
1095 and not act like the bird catcher
who calls and attracts the bird
with sweetness until he has it in his net,
then kills it and destroys it and plucks it.
Lady, your eyes, brighter than a star,
1100 look, as he does not hide his heart from you,
at your servant who loves you so much.
To God and to you he complains.
A thousand times, welcome!
Great joy has grown in my heart

102 La Cort d'Amor

1105 qar es tant fina e tant liaus.
Ja mos cors non haura repaus
tro qe·m digas coment sera
si'll vostre bel cors m'amera.
Q'ieu soi vostr'hom en tota guisza,
1110 qe Fin'Amor el cor m'atisza
un fuec don m'es suaus la flama,
qe del vostre bel cors m'aflama.
E regardatz lo vostr'honor,
qe diguen li fin'amador
1115 q'en vos non sap om blasmar re
qe bella es e de gran merce.
De paur no·us aus dire pus,
mais vostr'amor mi don Christus,
aissi con ieu, per bona fe,
1120 l'aus qerer, (mi)don', e·l (de)vos[tre] be.
Q'ieu no·m puesc ges de vos defendre,
enguazar mi podes o vendre.
Faitz en faire cartas e brieus,
mon* cors prenc de vos e mos fieus,
1125 e qar eu soi sener d'amor
hai causit lo pus ric seinhor.'
   [L]i lors respon : 'Eu(a)* soi ben vostra,
q'ieu non soi ges aqil* qe mostra
orguell mentre q'es iovencella
1130 q'a la color fresca e novella,
e qant aqil colors li fail
ez el se ve(i) en son mirail,
e conois qe trop s'es tarzada,
ill qier so don era pregada
1135 e ditz: "Ben hai mon tenps perdut:
jamais non poirai haver drut'.
Adoncs oing sa cara e la freta,
e cuida se faire toseta.
E on pus se gensa, e·l peizura
1140 qe·l beutat non ven per natura.
Qe domnas i ha d'autre fuel,
qe paron laide, ande non vuel

fol. 41ᵛ col. 1

1124 MS *mos*   1127 MS *ela*   1128 MS *aqel*

1105 for you are so fine and so loyal.
I will never be at ease
until you tell me how it will be
if your beautiful person loves me.
For I am your man in all ways,
1110 since True Love kindles a fire
in my heart whose flame is gentle to me,
for he has set me alight with your lovely person.
Have regard to your honour,
so that the true lovers may say
1115 that one can condemn nothing in you
for you are beautiful and most merciful.
From fear, I dare not tell you more,
but may Christ grant me your love
and your good, as I, in good faith,
1120 dare to seek it, lady.
Since I certainly cannot put up any resistance
against you, you can engage me or sell me.
Have charters and documents made
that I hold my self and my fiefs from you,
1125 and as I am the lord of love
I have chosen the most splendid overlord.'
　　She replies to him: 'I am surely yours,
for I am certainly not the [kind of] woman who shows
pride whilst she is a young lady
1130 with a fresh new colour,
and when this colour abandons her
and she looks at herself in the mirror
and realizes that she has delayed too long,
she seeks that for which she had been beseeched
1135 and says: "I have certainly wasted my time:
[now] I never will be able to have a lover".
Then she anoints her face and rubs it,
and thinks she can make herself into a young girl [again].
And the more she decorates herself, the worse she makes it
1140 since the beauty is not natural.
For there are ladies of another sort,
who appear unseemly, and I do not desire

qe negus gentils hom si fi
en dompna qe laidura di.
1145 Ant sse devont d'aitant veniar,
qe francs hom non la deu baiszar.
Dompna non deu parlar mas gent
e suau e causidament,
e deu tant gent sos motz assire
1150 qe totz hom son solaz desire,
qe las paraulas qe son fors
demostran los talens del cors.
Per qe non deu dire folor,
dompna qe s'enten en valor.'
1155 [L]a Baillessa d'Amor s'assis   col. 2
davant las pulsellas e dis:
'Sabetz qe deu faire doncella
qant sos bos amicx es ab ella,
e Fin'Amors l'a tant onrada
1160 q'ab son bon amic l'a colgada?
Lor coven q'al comensamen
li fassa d'un baisar presen,
e pueis ab rire ez ab solaz
qe·l faissa coisin de son braz
1165 ez ab l'autre ves si l'estrenia
e diga·s: "Grans onors vos venia,
amors, e gran[s] bon'aventura!
Fols es qe de vos se rancura,
qe s'anc me venc maltrac de vos
1170 bon[s] m'en es rendutz gazardos.
Bels amics, vos podes veder
q'ieu soi tota al vostre plazer,
qe vesetz qe no·m gard de vos
e vos es tan bels e tan bos
1175 qe gardaretz de vilania
vo[s]tre bel cors e vostra amia.
Endreit vos non desir lo rei.
Al vostre causiment m'autrei
e vos sabetz qe de toseta
1180 no i·ha onor cel qe l'abeta.

that any gentleman should trust
in a lady who says unseemly things.
1145 Rather, they must have such revenge,
that a noble man will not kiss her.
A lady must only speak nobly
and gently and appropriately,
and must place her words so nobly
1150 that every man desire her conversation,
for the external words
show the desires inside the body.
Which is why a lady must not speak
folly if she aspires to merit.'
1155 The Bailiff of Love sat down
in front of the maidens and said:
'Do you know what a young lady should do
when her close companion is with her,
and True Love has honoured her so much
1160 that he has let her sleep with her close companion?
It befits them that first
she should bestow a kiss upon him
and then, with a smile and sweet words,
let her make a cushion for him of her arm
1165 and with the other clasp him to her
and say this: "May great honour come to you,
my love, and much good fortune!
Foolish is he who complains about you,
for if ever I suffered on account of you,
1170 I have received ample recompense for it.
Handsome companion, you can see
that I am totally at your disposal,
for you see that I do not keep myself from you
and you are so handsome and so good
1175 that you will keep your handsome self
and your beloved from uncouthness.
I do not desire the king in your place.
I yield myself to your discretion
and you know that he who tricks
1180 a young girl has no honour.

Gran maltrait hai per vos haiut:
soven n'hai lo maniar perdut
e quant eu cuiava dormir
m'esvellavon li dous sospir,
1185 qe pensava, bels amicx dous,
. . . .
e quant eu era residada,
disia: 'Mala fui anc nada,
Seinher Dieus, qar non dura totz tenps
q'adoncs sivals estiam emsens,
1190 eu e mos amicx per cui plor.
Non puesc pus soffretar l'ardor
q'Amors m'auci de fina enveia.'
Mais ia non er qe Dieus non veia,
amis, se vos m'aves traïda
1195 q'ie·us hai de mon poder servida.
Non faissaz lo lairon qe di,
qant s'encontra ab lo pellegri:
'De savis tenez, bels amics.
Savis es vostre dreit[z] camis!',
1200 e quant l'a mes el bois preont,
li tol son aver e·l confont.
Amics, non si'eu confonduda
atressi, car vos hai seguda.
Davant m'estava ben e gent,
1205 mais era perd lo cor e·l sen.
Non puesc pus la dolor suffrir
qi·m fai la color laideszir.
Aqest mal hai haiut per vos,
amics, e Dieus q'es francs e bos
1210 e pius e plens de corteszia
sab qe·us hai amat ses bauszia.
E vuella q'entre mi e vos
vivam lonc tenps ez amen nos.
Tenes lo man q'eu vos o jur,
1215 ez enaisi vos asegur,
qe za totz los iorns de ma vida
no·us farai de m'amor genchida.
E vos iuras m'o atressi
qe non fassas lo bel mati

fol. 42ʳ col. 1

col. 2

Through you I have had great pain;
often I have lost my appetite as a result
and when I thought I would sleep
sweet sighs kept me awake,
1185 for I was thinking, sweet handsome companion
. . . .
and when I had woken up,
I said: 'I wish I had never been born,
Lord God, since it [my dream] does not last,
for then at least we were together,
1190 I and my companion on account of whom I cry.
No longer can I support the ardour
for Love kills me with pure desire.'
But it will not happen that God shall not see,
my love, if you have betrayed me,
1195 for I have served you with all my strength.
Do not imitate the robber who says,
when he encounters a pilgrim:
'Go wisely, fine friend.
Wise is your straight path!',
1200 and when he has got him in the depths of the wood,
takes his possessions and kills him.
My love, may I not die
in the same way because I have followed you.
It used to please and content me,
1205 but now I have lost spirit and judgement.
I can no longer support the grief
which makes my complexion grow ugly.
I have had this ill through you,
my love, and God who is noble and good
1210 and pious and full of courtliness
knows that I have loved you without deceit.
May he desire that both you and I
may live a long time and love each other.
Hold my hand so that I may swear to you,
1215 and thus assure you,
that every day of my life
I will not refuse you my love.
And you, swear to me in the same way
that you shall not imitate the fine morning

108 LA CORT D'AMOR

1220 qe tramet el miez luec del iorn
la plueia e·l vent e·l tenps morn."
Ez el responda qe cortes:
"Dompna, ben conosch qe dretz es
e dic vos per los sans qe son,
1225 qe tant qant viurai en est mon
non amarai autre mas vos,
ni a present ni a rescos.
Amors e Ious si iug[n]irent
mi e vos d'aqest convinent.
1230 Aissi con son bon e privat
vuellon qe tengam lialtat
e q'entre nos non haia engan.
A Dieu et a vos mi coman;
e baisem nous enqar cove
1235 e nom de tota bona fe."
Enaissi deu esser segura   *fol. 42^V col. 1*
dompna de drut, si i met sa cura.
E quant ve<u>n</u>ra* al departir,
sitot lor es mal a sufrir
1240 cant abhora s'adobes li
e parta de lui tant mati,
qe za non sapcha mals ni bos
mais coma ssi anc re non fo(u)s.
E sapchia mesatje causir
1245 qe la(p) sapchia tan gen cubrir
qe paraula* sia cellada
q'hom non sapcha qant n'er tornada.
El mati, si ve(i) en la plasa
son amic, ia semb[l]an non fasa
1250 q'anc enqera no·l veges,
ni qe sapcha de lui qi es,
qe·l ious d'amor fruita e floris,
qi ab sen lo garda e·l nouris.'
[L]a cortesa vallen Valors
1255 enseina e <u>d</u>itz* als amadors:

1238 MS *uerra*
1246 MS *pauraula*. There are two expunctuation dots under the first *u*.
1255 MS *eclitz*

1220 which at midday sends
rain and wind and bleak weather."
And let him reply like a courtly man:
"Lady, well I know that it is just,
and I tell you by all the saints there are,
1225 that as long as I live in this world
I will love no other but you,
neither openly nor in private.
Love and Joy thus joined
you and me by this agreement.
1230 Just as they are good and intimate
they desire that we may preserve loyalty
and that there may be no deceit between us.
To God and to you I commend myself;
and let us kiss each other, whilst it is fitting
1235 in the name of all good faith."
Thus should a lady be reassured
by her lover if she is concerned about this.
And when it comes to leaving,
although it is hard for them to bear
1240 that she should get dressed there so early
and leave him so early,
let her not feel pleased or displeased
any more than if nothing had ever happened there.
And may she know how to choose a messenger
1245 who is able to keep her secret so well
and whose speech is [so] discreet
that no one may know when she returns.
In the morning, if she sees her companion
in the square, let her certainly not show
1250 that she has ever seen him before,
nor that she knows who he is,
for the joy of love fruits and blossoms
for whoever minds and feeds it with judgement.'
  The courteous and noble Merit
1255 instructs and addresses the lovers:

110 *La Cort d'Amor*

'Mult deu esser vallens e pros
totz hom pois se feing am**o**ros*,
des qe pois ha vist los bels mans
de sidons, per qe pur es* villans,
1260 qe prous dompna ab fresca color
es ruesa del vergier(s) d'Amor.
E deu prenre de ch(i)ausiment
tant de leis e d'enseinhament   *col. 2*
c'om digua: "Ben tenc per onrada
1265 la dompna don aqest s'agrada,
e cill qe l'ama a ben causit
pro drut e vallent e ardit
e homen q'ades se mellura.
En bon lou ha tornat sa cura!"
1270 Apress fasa tant de proessa
qe sa dompna franca e cortesza
parle privadamens ab lui.
Qe qant ill seran ambedui
emsens, mout dousament li diga:
1275 "Dieus vos sal, bella dousa amiga,
co**m**a* la pus ben ensenhada
e la genszer q'anc fos amada!
E pos Dieus ha en vos tramessa
honor e beutat e franqessa,
1280 merces no·n sia ia ostada.
Amors, eu pert tanta velada,
e per tant angoissus martire
m'es(en)menda, q'ella·m vuella rire,
o qe la dousa man del gan
1285 me lais baiszar en sospiran.
Bella dompna, vostra faissos
me fai ardit e paoros.
Non soi ben arditz q'en tal loc
ausei qerre solas ni ioc.
1290 Mei uell non s'auszon enardir   *fol. 43ʳ col. 1*
d'esgardar, tro qe·m sen murir.

1257 MS *amaros*
1259 MS *puʳes*. A small superscript *r* has been added over the back half of the *u*. In fact, it is written unclearly and could equally be a *c*.
1276 MS *cona*

'Most noble and worthy must every man
be once he aspires to be a lover,
once he has seen the beautiful messages
of his lady, on account of which the base man is purified,
1260 for a worthy lady with a fresh complexion
is a rose in the garden of Love.
He must choose
such laws and teaching
that one may say: "Greatly honoured I hold
1265 the lady in whom this man takes pleasure,
and she who loves him has certainly chosen
a worthy, noble and bold lover
and a man who constantly improves himself.
She has turned her attention to a good place!"
1270 Then let him perform such deeds of merit
that his pure and courtly lady
may speak with him in private.
And when they are both
together, let him say to her sweetly:
1275 "God save you, beautiful and sweet love,
as the best instructed
and the most gracious who was ever loved!
And since God has endowed you with
honour and beauty and nobility,
1280 may mercy never be withdrawn.
Love, I lose so many sleepless nights,
so compensate me for this bitter agony,
let her want to smile at me
or allow me to kiss, sighing,
1285 the sweet hand of her glove.
Beautiful lady, your face
makes me bold and afraid.
I am not so bold that in such a place
I dared to seek conversation or play.
1290 May my eyes not be so bold
as to look [at you], until I feel myself dying.

112 LA CORT D'AMOR

Adoncs vos esgar de paor
com lo s<u>e</u>rs* son irat seinhor,
qe non l'ausza merce clamar,
1295 mais plora e pensa: 'S'ieu l'esgar,
ades l'en venra pietatz
qant veira lo gran dol q'eu fatz'.
Ja non aurai ioi ni salut
tro qe vostre bel cors m'aiut,
1300 qe, per ma fe, trop m'es pus bon,
qe·m prometaz, q'altra mi don.
Bella dousa res cui reblan,
totz tenps vos semblarai l'enfan
qe plora per la bella re
1305 totas las oras q'el la ve
entro qe·l ha. Aital farai
e si no·us puesc haver, morrai.
E diran totz qant m'aures mort:
'Sa dompna l'aucis a grant tort,
1310 mais sals er al dia del iuzizi
qe mort es per son bel servizi'.
Grans merces vos clama vostre sers,
qe per vos lo ten en gras fers
don zamais non sera fors
1315 tro qe l'en get vostre bels cors.
Ses engan e ses cor volatje
m'autrei el vostre seinhoratje.   *col. 2*
Las mans iointas a genolos,
a Deu me coman et a vos.
1320 Q'anc pos vos me donestes jorn,
non estet mos cors en soiorn;
antz, se Dieus de vos m'aconsel,
hai pregat la luna e·l solel,
e dreig, coma <u>mos</u> <u>bons</u>* seinors,
1325 per Dieu, que·m breugesson lo[s] <u>i</u>ors*
q'ieu vos volia vezer tan
q'us pauchs jorns me scemblava un an.
Ja per mal qe·m fassas suffrir
no·m laissarai de vos servir.

1293 MS *sors*   1324 MS *bons mos*   1325 MS *cors*

THE COURT OF LOVE

So I look at you fearfully
as the servant does his angry lord,
and does not dare to beg for mercy
1295 but cries and thinks: 'If I look at him,
pity will immediately come from him
when he sees the great sorrow that I have'.
Never will I have joy or health
until your beautiful person helps me,
1300 for, by my faith, it is much more pleasing to me that
you should promise me [something] than that another should
    give me [something].
Beautiful and sweet creature whom I serve,
to you I will always seem a child
who cries for a beautiful object
1305 all the while that he sees it
until he has it. Thus will I act
and will die if I cannot have you.
And when you have killed me all will say:
'His lady killed him most grievously,
1310 but he will be saved on Judgement Day
because he died through his fine service'.
Your servant asks for great mercy from you
for on account of you he is held in great irons
from which he will never escape
1315 until your beautiful person frees him.
Without deceit and without a fickle heart
I yield myself to your power.
With joined hands and on my knees,
I commend myself to God and to you.
1320 For ever since you gave me a rendez-vous,
I have not been at ease;
rather, God help me,
I have beseeched the moon and the sun,
face to face, as my good lords,
1325 for God's sake, that they might shorten the days for me
as I wanted to see you so much
that a short day seemed a year to me.
Even with any pain you may make me suffer
I will never leave off serving you.

114   LA CORT D'AMOR

1330 A la gran valor et al sen
 ez al bel cors de vos mi ren."'
 [Pos] que ja si* ha parlat Valors,
 auien totz l'en merceia Amors.
 Apres lui comencet Proessa
1335 e dis: 'Eu no·m soi entremessa
 ad aqesta cort(z) de parlar;
 ez hai auzit a totz comtar,
 per Crist, bonas raszos e bellas;
 mais eu vos comtarai novellas,
1340 qe no·s taignon ges entre vos,
 qe fan li fol drut nuailos.
 Q'ara venra per aventura
 (un) drutz enqer[re] bon'avetura,
 el ious de fin'amor entratz.   fol. 43ᵛ col. 1
1345 Ez ira qerre son solatz
 a dompna q'ez (er) coinda e joiousa,
 e trobara la angoisosa
 e comensera a rogir
 . . . .
 et il fara o de talant.
1350 E ben leu respondra·l aitant:
 "Amicx, vos non sabetz ab cui
 parlatz, c'anc vos ni autrui
 non amei, ni non sai qe s'es.
 Mais si eu m'en entremeses,
1355 vos* es ben tan bels e tan pros
 q'ieu fera mon amic de vos.
 E si voletz haver mon grat
 ins aisi on es comensat,
 si fasat[z] q'eu vos n'encus,*
1360 qe per lo mens ni per lo pus,
 non er fachs e dic vilania
 qar eu non esdevent vostra amia."
 Ez el pa[r]tra s'en vergoinos,
 e·l dompna q'es valents e pros

1332 MS q=jasi [?]. The start of this line is bizarrely written. There are two
 horizontal lines connecting the q to the j, which I can only take to be an
 attempt to reproduce as well as possible an illegible written model. See
 also the note to this line.
1355 MS ves   1359 MS si lasat qeu uos uencus

1330 To your great worth and judgement,
and to your beautiful person, I deliver myself."'
Once Merit has spoken thus,
in the hearing of all Love thanks him for it.
After him Prowess began
1335 and said: 'I did not come
to this court in order to speak;
and I have heard all relate,
in the name of Christ, good and fine discourses;
but I will relate tales to you,
1340 which are scarcely suitable in your presence,
about what foolish, indolent lovers do.
For perchance a lover who has donned
the yoke of true love
will now come and seek good fortune.
1345 He will seek his solace
with a lady who is charming and joyous,
and will find her distressed
and she will start to blush
. . . .
and she will do it with desire.
1350 She will readily reply thus to him:
"Companion, you do not know with whom
you are speaking, for never did I love you
or any other, nor do I know what it is [to love].
But if I were to undertake it,
1355 you are certainly so handsome and so worthy
that I would make you my companion.
And if you want to have my good will
in here [in my heart] where it began,
then ensure that I should not accuse you
1360 that in absolutely any way
will uncouthness ever be done or said
because I do not become your partner."
And he will depart from her ashamed,
and the lady who is worthy and excellent

1365 tenra lo per avilanit
e dira: "Ben valra petit
aquela qe vos amara!
Mais valriatz ad ermita,
vos es be d'aqel lignatje
1370 don son li fol drut salvatje!"
E vechs la bon'amor perduda *col. 2*
qar non es qi l'aia seguda
qe drutz i ha qe per folor
demandon o qeran amor.
1375 Qe ben sapchatz que eu amaria
volenters si trobes amia.
Venga sai cel qe vol amar,
q'ieu sai q'el en potra trobar
qe s'el i vol metre s'ententa,
1380 s'el ne vol una, en haura trenta.
De drut conven q'al comensar
en prec tan o fassa pregar
tro qe s'avenga e s'eschaja
en pro dompna valent e gaia.
1385 E si non la pot tan tost trobar,
ges per so no·s deu esfredar,
qe cel qe cercha l'aur tant lava
lo lot e trastorna la grava
tro qe truoba lo luzant aur
1390 don es rics e don fai tesaur.
Per qe non deu haver nuala,
qe precs e servir[s] e trabala,
s'era del mon la pus estraigna,
si li·n fara dousa compaigna.
1395 Ez apres q'aiha tal messatje,
q'el diga e·l man son coratje
a cellas q'han d'amor talan,
mas bellament e ses malan. *fol. 44ʳ col. 1*
E trobera aitant d'aqelas
1400 com le cels pod haver estelas,
q'una non trobares a dire
qi no am lo solaz e·l rire
d'amor, si noncha vol lo pus.
E diga: "Ja no·m sal Christus

1365	will consider him abased
	and will say: "She will be worth very little,
	she who loves you!
	You would be worth more to an anchoress,
	you are certainly of that lineage
1370	to which foolish wild lovers belong!"
	And there you see good love lost
	because there is no one who has followed it
	for there are lovers who ask for
	or strive after love through folly.
1375	For well you know that I would love
	willingly, if I found a lady friend.
	Let any man who wishes to love come here,
	for I know that he will be able to find it,
	for if he is willing to devote his efforts to it,
1380	if he wants one, he will have thirty.
	For a lover it is fitting that at first
	he beseeches so much or has her beseeched
	until it comes about and it is fitting
	for a worthy, noble and joyful lady.
1385	And if he cannot find her so quickly,
	he must not lose heart at all on that account,
	for he who seeks gold washes
	the mud so much and turns over the sand
	until he finds the sparkling gold
1390	with which he is rich and of which he makes his treasure.
	Which is why he must not be indolent,
	for prayers and service and torture,
	even if it is the cruellest in the world,
	will still bring him sweet company.
1395	And then let him have such a messenger,
	who may speak and announce his feelings on his behalf
	to those who desire love,
	minding it is eloquent and without wickedness.
	He will surely find as many of those
1400	as the sky can have stars,
	for you will not find a single woman
	who does not love the conversation and laughter
	of love, even if she does not want the rest.
	Let him say: "May Christ not save me

1405 s'ieu non sai, bella dompna e bona,
qi porta de Ioi la corona
sobre lo(u)s amadors del mon.
E vos baiszares* m'en lo fron
senpres qant eu lo vos dirai.
1410 Qe lo joventz q'en vos estai*
e·l vergoigna qi ren non tria
vos en fara faire folia
q'el n'es be de xx. parts semos.
Mais eu lo lauzava a vos
1415 e dic vos qe sots lo solel
non haura bazaler parel.
Ben seriatz de ioi la soma.
De dous arbre ch(i)ai dousa poma,
. . . .
q'ambedui es molt avinent.
1420 A! Com se* conten ricament!
Qe s'el vol haver bon solatz
ja hom non sera enoiatz,
e quant es ab sabia gen
los ap(r)odera totz de sen.
1425 Anc els mieus zorns non fo tan bos *col. 2*
ni tan bels tan pauc orguolos.
Eu sai q'ins el cor vos sab bon
so q'eu dic; e si dizes non,
eu sai qe vos non dizes ver.
1430 E·uz metrai aisz e lezer
e progarai tan lo sejnor,
si Dieus plaz, vos dara i s'amor.
E si tant fatz qe·l bel[s] e·l bon[s]
vos ame, lo mieus gazardon[s]
1435 non sia ges mes en oblit,
q'ie·us darai gran re per petit.
Q'ieu lo mogui l'altre[r] de loin
per saber si n'hauria soin,

1408 MS *bauszares*   1410 MS *estaz*
1420 MS *sa*. The end of *conten* is unclear, and looks like *conteit* which has then been corrected by joining the top of the *i* to the *t*.

1405 if I do not know, beautiful and good lady,
who wears the crown of Joy
above all the lovers in the world.
You will kiss my brow
immediately when I tell you who it is.
1410 For the youth that is in you
and your undiscerning sense of decency
will make you behave foolishly
so that he is condemned a good twenty times.
But I was recommending him to you
1415 and I tell you that under the sun
there will never be such a youth again.
You would certainly be the zenith of joy.
A sweet apple falls from a sweet tree,
. . . .
which is greatly agreeable to both of them.
1420 Ah! How splendidly he behaves here!
For if he desires fine conversation
no one will ever be bored,
and when he is with wise people
he will surpass them all in judgement.
1425 Never was there such a good man in my days,
nor such a handsome one who was so little proud.
I know that in your heart what I say
is pleasing to you; and if you say no,
I know that you are not telling the truth.
1430 But I will give you an occasion and an opportunity
    [to meet with him]
and I will beseech my lord in such a way that,
if it pleases God, he will give you his love there.
And if I do so much that the handsome, good man
loves you, do not
1435 forget my reward,
for I will give you a great thing in return for a small one.
For the other day I tentatively sounded him out
to know if he would care about it,

120 *LA CORT D'AMOR*

   e i dis, ses vostre saubut,
1440 qe vos li mandavatz salut.
   E qant el s'auzi saludar
   de part vos, non poc mais sonar
   d'una pessa, pueis respondet:
   'C. milia merces li ret
1445 con de sson sers endompneiatz.
   Ab son rire·m teing per pagatz,
   anc mais non entremis d'amor,
   e aqesta·m fai gran paor
   qe m'ausi ab un dous esgart,
1450 qe dompnas han en l'uel dart
   ab qe naffron tan dousament
   qe mentre q'hom mor non o sent, *fol. 44ᵛ col. 1*
   qe·l gai* cors ausi drut cortes
   com lo roissinol qant es pres
1455 qe non pot esser ab sa par.
   Per qe vai a midons pregar,
   si com ell'es francha e cortesza,
   non per me mais per gentilesza
   m'acuella, qe sos ser[s] se mor
1460 si no me garofla·l cor,
   ab un baiszar, sa dousa alena
   q'enaissi·m pot gitar de pena.'
   Lo zou[s] de vos me fai plorar.
   Quant eu lo vi color mudar,
1465 qar conogui a son scenblan
   qe·us amaria ses engan,
   aitant n'hai comensat ses vos.
   Amatz lo, qe bels es e bos,
   e no·l fassatz la vilania
1470 qe fan las dompnas per folia
   qi·s fan pregar un an o dos,
   q'ez aqell pregar enojos,
   qe cuzon qe lur onor sia,
   lur tol lor pretz e·l desenbria."
1475 [L]a dompna dira: "No·us mais pes.
   Sembla qe·l faz vos trameses,

1453 MS *gaz*

THE COURT OF LOVE 121

and I said to him, without your knowledge,
1440 that you sent him your greeting.
When he heard himself greeted
by you, he could no longer speak
for a while, then he replied:
'I send her one hundred thousand thanks
1445 as if from her bondsman.
With her smile I consider myself paid,
I never asked for anything more from love,
and this lady makes me greatly afraid
that she will kill me with a sweet look,
1450 since ladies have a dart in their eyes
with which they wound so sweetly
that whilst a man is dying he does not feel it,
for the joyful lady kills the courtly lover
like the nightingale when it is caught
1455 and cannot be with its partner.
Which is why I am going to beseech my lady whether,
since she is so noble and courtly,
she may not welcome me on my account
but through goodness, for her servant will die
1460 if her sweet breath does not indeed perfume
my heart with a kiss,
for thus can she save me from pain.'
The yoke he bears on your account makes me weep.
When I saw him change colour,
1465 because I recognized from his appearance
that he would love you without deceit,
I initiated this much without you.
Love him, for he is handsome and good,
and do not behave ungraciously with him
1470 like the ladies who behave foolishly
and let themselves be beseeched for a year or two,
for it is this tiresome beseeching,
that they think is to their honour,
which removes their worth and diminishes it."
1475   The lady will say: "Do not let this concern you any more.
It seems that the foolish man sends you,

e per mesatje[s] logaditz
fan mantas dompnas fols arditz,
e·n son rep[re]szas e traïdas.
1480 Ben hai vostras raszos auzidas
e quant eu lo porai vezer
eu sabrai si vos dizes ver,
qe s'ieu parle veszent la gent
ab lui, fols es qe m'en repren."
1485 "[D]ompna, ben sai qe pels truans,
qe fan las fa[u]las e·ls engans,
son li bon homen mescreszut;
mais, dompna, si Dieus ja m'azut,
sitot me soi de paubra gent,
1490 lial homen son miei parent
ez eu soi de lur parenta[t]
. . . .
Q'ieu vos dic, bella dompna e genta,
qe si vos en fiz(av)az en me,
eu vos [d]irai per bona fe
1495 q'el vos amara e vos lui,
q'ieu vei* qe morez ambedui
d'amor. Or(us) vos non sentez* re,
mai si vos vos veiziatz* be,
a la color q'havetz perduda,
1500 vos diriatz: 'Por Deu, m'ajuda
q'el me am!'. Non digas oc ni no,
q'ieu parlarai oimais d'aiso
e farai vos la pus onrada
dompna de tot'esta contrada."
1505   [L]a do[m]pna dira: "To[s]t veirai
a qual part vostre cor metrai:
en engan on en liautat.
Si m'enganatz, farez pecat."
  "[D]ompna, ans percas lo vostre be.
1510   No m'en crezes, vec vos ma fe,
q'ieu i regarde vostra* onor.
Maldit sion li traïdor

col. 2

fol. 45ʳ col. 1

1496 MS *vez*   1497 MS *sintez*   1498 MS *veizzatz*   1511 MS *vostre*

and on account of hired messengers
many ladies commit foolish acts of boldness,
and are condemned and deceived on account of it.
1480 Carefully have I heard your arguments
and when I am able to see him
I will know if you are telling the truth,
and if I speak to him in the sight
of all, foolish is he who reproaches me for it."
1485 "Lady, well I know that because of the rascals
who tell tall stories and do deceitful things,
good men are doubted;
but, my lady, God help me,
although I am of poor lineage,
1490 my family are loyal people
and I am of their line
. . . .
For I tell you, beautiful and noble lady,
that if you trust me in this matter,
I will tell you in good faith
1495 that he will love you and you him,
for I see that you are both dying
of love. Now you notice nothing,
but if you examine yourself closely,
you would say to the colour
1500 you have lost: 'For God's sake, help me
so that he may love me!'. Do not say yes or no,
for I will speak of this in the future
and will make you the most honoured
lady of all this region."
1505 The lady will say: "I shall soon see
where I will classify your heart:
in deceit or in loyalty.
If you deceive me you will be committing a sin."
"Lady, I seek, on the contrary, your profit.
1510 If you do not believe me, here I pledge to you
that I have regard to your honour in this matter.
May the traitors be cursed

       qe per lur soi mescrezuda.
       Anseis fos ma lenga perduda
1515 q'ie·us hages dit mas so qe·s taing.
       Si tant fatz q'ieu vos acompaing
       ab lui, una causa vos dic:
       Amatz lo mais c'Aia Landric!
       E qe val qant viu ses amor
1520 dompna q'es de vostra valor.
       Tot es vostra color mudada:
       eu cug qe vos es soclamada,
       qe·l frons vos no·s gieta calor.
       Non es: anz es lo mal[s] d'amor
1525 qe·us ha tenguda* longament.
       Mo[r]ta es qi consol no i prent!
       Ja vostra mort non soffrirai*:
       a Dieu vos coman. Vau m'en lai
       pregar lo franc e·l amoros.
1530 E si tant fai* q'el parl'a vos,
       non li siatz ges preszenteira
       mais vergoinosa e pauc parleira.
       E on pus seres enveiosa   *col. 2*
       de lui, feines [vos] vergoinosa,
1535 mais no·l laises ges s'a[fa]mar
       a re q'el sapchia demandar.
       Q'adorar deu hom e grazir
       dompna, qan sab gen acuelir.
       S'ieu podia aiso acabar,
1540 mais cuiaria conquistar
       qe s'era oultra mar romeva.
       Ja negus om no m'en don trieva
       qi volra vostra amor blasmar,
       mais venga·n a mi parlar.
1545 Q'ambedui es molt avinent,
       bel et enfant e covinent,
       e tota gens la lausaria,
       la vostra amor, si la sabia;
       per estiers non er za saubut,
1550 ni ja·l veszin no·n faran brut,

1525 MS *cenguda*   1527 MS *soffriraz*   1530 MS *faz*

for on their account am I doubted.
It would have been better for me to lose my tongue
1515 than to have said anything except what is fitting.
If you go so far as to let me go with you
to him, I tell you one thing:
Love him more than Aia did Landric!
What is a lady of your merit
1520 worth if she lives without love?
Your complexion has entirely changed:
I think you are feverish
for your brow does not emit heat.
You are not: rather is it love-sickness
1525 which has held you for a long time.
Dead is she who does not take advice!
I shall certainly not let you die:
I commend you to God. I go away to that place [where he is]
to beseech that sincere and amorous man.
1530 And if I succeed in arranging for him to speak to you,
do not be at all forward,
but shy and not very talkative.
The more you desire
him, pretend to be shy,
1535 but certainly do not let him die of hunger
for something that he could ask for.
For a man must adore and praise
a lady when she knows how to receive him well.
If I could achieve this,
1540 I would think I had overcome more
than if I had gone on a pilgrimage overseas.
Indeed, let no man give me a truce
who wants to condemn your love,
but let him come to speak to me about it.
1545 For you are both very agreeable,
handsome, young and well-formed,
and everyone would praise
your love if they knew about it;
besides, neither will it be known,
1550 nor will the neighbours ever gossip about it,

ni non sabra hom vostr'afaire
mais nos tres q'em coma fraire,
ez Amors qi fara lo qart
qi nos gitara de regart.'
1555 E qant venra al avesprar
veigna tot son senor comdar
qant haura lo zorn s'espleitat.
Ja anseis non sia laisat
tro qe s'eschiaza a fin'amor,
1560 puis am ses cor galiador.'
[Q]ant Proessa hag dit son agrat,
l'amador son en pes levat
e fetz caschus a si dons un gin.
Adoncs foron uberts escrin
1565 e joas donadas e preszas
qi non son ges en perdos meszas
q'hom non sap lo prez adismar;
cor e deszir e dous esgar
e plaszer, cug cil q'ho demanda,
1570 e baiszar ab q'Amors abranda
lo coratje dels fis amans
e lur fai faire sos comans.
Ad Amor han dig en rient:
'Nos volem nostre convinent,
1575 seiner, e per onor de vos,
dansar veian vostres baros'.
Amors lur o ha autrezatz
e apres lur ha comandatz:
'Anatz suau e bellament,
1580 e cantatz clar et* aut e gent!'.
Trenta cofres totz ples de flors
lor fetz per sol gitar Amors,
qe fez traïre de son tesaur
q'el no i ten argent ni aur.
1585 Ni non toca aur ni argent
si non sei joias q'hom no vent,
qe non son ges per aur gardadas,
ans son per Fin'Amor baiszadas

fol. 45ᵛ col. 1

col. 2

1580 MS æt

nor will anyone know about your affair
but the three of us, who are like brothers,
and Love, who will constitute the fourth,
and who will keep us out of danger."
1555 And when it starts to get dark
let him come and tell his lord all about
what he has accomplished that day.
Indeed, may things not be left undone
until he is judged fitting for true love,
1560 since he loves without a treacherous heart.'
    When Prowess had spoken his pleasure,
    the lovers stood up
and each gave his lady a sign.
Then the jewellery cases were opened
1565 and jewels were given and taken
that are not at all wasted
for one would not be able to estimate their price:
[they are worth] heart and desire and sweet looks
and pleasure, thinks he who asks this,
1570 and kissing with which Love enflames
the heart of true lovers
and makes them follow his instructions.
To Love they said laughing:
'We desire our agreement,
1575 my lord, and in honour of you,
to dance in the sight of your barons'.
Love granted them this
and then ordered them:
'Go slowly and splendidly
1580 and sing distinctly, out loud and nobly!'.
Love had flowers, thirty chests full,
which he had had taken from his treasure,
for he does not keep silver or gold in it,
strewn across the floor.
1585 And he does not touch gold or silver
apart from six jewels which no one sells,
and are not at all guarded as if they were gold,
but rather are kissed by True Love

et envoutas de drap de seda.
1590 Plaçers faire sensa moneda,
ses tot aver, fai sa fazenda.
Q'el ha tot qant se vol de renda,
qe tot qant tenon l'amirant
ni·l rei, tot es a sson comant.
1595 Ni negun denier non adesa
qar dompnas en fan cobeesa.
Cascus drutz si dons la flor lansa.
Do[m]pneis se vai penre en la dansa,
q'es adretz et ag cor isnel,
1600 e porta cascus un capel
de ruesza, pueis dis en rizent:
'Amors, fols es qi se deffent
e qui totz los jorns* de sa via
non es en vostra seinhoria.
1605 Qi apres aiso au los sons
e·ls novels motz de las chansons
e regarda la gran coindia
qe cascus drutz fai ab s'amia,
e los dous rires* e·ls solatz
1610 e·ls gins e los baiszars enblatz
e las frescas colors qe·l hant,
e la beutat q'en lor resplant
e las bellas crins entreszadas
. . . .
ben es sers e plens de felonia   *fol. 46ʳ col. 1*
1615 qi ves Amor(s) non s'umilia.'
[L]i baron han Amor pregat,
per Dieu, qe·l bal sion laisat
qe non podon lo zou soffrir
qar ab pauc non volon morir
1620 qant lur soven de las onradas
. . . .
qe non auszon far bel semblant
a lur drutz com aqestas fant.
[A]mors comandet a Plaszer
qe las fassa tornar sezer

1603 MS *jonrs*   1609 MS *cires*

and wrapped in silk cloth.
1590 To bring pleasures without money,
without any possession, is his business.
For he has all the recompense he wants,
for all that the emirs and the kings
own is at his command.
1595 And he does not touch any coin
because ladies behave covetously as a result [if he does].
Each lover throws his lady a flower.
Love Service, who is just and has a
quick heart, goes to join the dance,
1600 and everyone wears a crown
of roses, then he says laughing:
'Love, foolish is he who deprives himself
and who is not in your power
all the days of his life.
1605 Anyone who after this hears the tunes
and the new words of the songs
and sees the great charm
that each lover shows his lady,
the sweet laughter and the conversation
1610 and the furtive glances and the stolen kisses,
the fresh complexions they have,
the beauty that shines in them
and their beautiful plaited hair
. . . .
he is certainly a serf and full of treachery
1615 if he does not humble himself before Love.'
    The barons have beseeched Love,
for God's sake, that the ball be abandoned
because they cannot bear the yoke
for they are not far from wanting to die
1620 when they remember the honoured women
. . . .
who do not dare receive their lovers
well as those women do.
    Love commanded Pleasure
that he should have them return to sit down

130 LA CORT D'AMOR

1625 e qe lur fassa bellament
ab drap de seda moure vent
o de l'aigua rosa gitar
en lur caras per reffrescar,
q'en la dansa han azut calor.
1630 Molt se do(mp)na gran soing de lor
e pueis ha dig: 'Za Dieus non veia,
cortesa gens, qe vos gerreia;
qe re non de[u] hom tant onrar
com bona dompna a fin amar.
1635 Mais per aqest mieu blonde cap,
be·m peszara s'Orguels non sap,
(e·l garsonala qu'el mante —
lo poder qe ha contra me)
qe za non er longa sazons
1640 qe l'en veran mil gonfanons,
qe volrian en un gran soil
dec lam areser, ab un oil*.
Q'ieu non voell soffrir la clamor
que fan dompnas e amador,
1645 e si vos, seinhor, m'o laissatz,
non lor er pus suffert en patz.'
[S]ens estet en un farestol
e plaz li molt qar Amors vol
gerrezar per tenir dreitura:
1650 el pensa qe sos fieus pejura;
e a·l dig: 'Anseis qe movatz
ad aqest besoing me sonatz,
e castias una folor
qe fan li fol drut feinedor.
1655 Qe qant ill ha sidons conqes,
. . . .
el se feing tan fort e s'aplaigna
q'el non cuida ges q'hom remaigna
en la villa qant el s'en eis,
e passa soen davan leis
1660 entro qe la gens en fai bruda*
e q'hom dis: "Aqella es sa druda".

col. 2

1642 MS *d e clamar.eser abun oil*   1660 MS *brada*

1625 and that he should have them delightfully
fanned with a cloth of silk
or rose water sprinkled
on their faces in order to refresh them,
for during the dance they had been hot.
1630 He concerns himself with them greatly
and then said: 'May God never see,
courtly people, anyone wage war on you;
for one must honour nothing as much
as a good lady does true love.
1635 But by this, my blond head,
it will weigh upon me greatly if Pride
(and the rabble he maintains—
the force he has against me)
does not know that it will certainly not be long
1640 before they [Pride and his rabble] will see a thousand banners
[emblazoned] with peacock eyes on a great battlefield,
intending to mock an imperfect vice.
For I do not want to endure the complaint
that the ladies and the lovers make,
1645 and if you give me leave, my lords,
it will no longer be peacefully tolerated from them.'
   Judgement was on a throne
   and it pleases him much that Love wants
to fight to maintain justice:
1650 he thinks that his fief is in decline;
and he says to him: 'Before you embark,
call me to assist in this cause,
and castigate a folly
that foolish presumptuous lovers perpetrate,
1655 for when they have conquered their lady,
. . . .
he puffs himself up so much and boasts
that he does not believe a single man remains
in the city when he leaves it,
and he often passes in front of her
1660 until people gossip about it
and one says: "That one is his mistress".

132   LA CORT D'AMOR

E el ten la bruit ad onor
e fa·n lo cer qe·l casador
e·l lebrier veinon ateignen
1665 ez el vai* s'en seguramen
e pot se denants tot garir,
e platz li tant qant (l)au glatir
los cans, qe torna e non sap mot
tro q'es mort e retegutz de tot.
1670 Aital fai* cel qe conzauzis
fol brut: si e sidonz traïs,
q'ans d(i)eu esser d'aital escuoil
qe s'amor[s] soisep tant son oil,
e·l fassa sidons esgardar,
1675 tost en deu la cara virar.
E folz semblantz torna a nient
amors e blasme de la gent,
e ben sapchiatz qe Malparler[s]
estai enaissi con l'archier[s]
1680 qe trai e naffra ab son qairel,
dementre qe canta, l'aucel;
atressi naffron l'enozos
malparler* los aman(i)s zoios
ab lor lengas, cui Dieus azir
1685 e los fan en viven murir!
Per qe·lz ne castias, bel seinher,
qe laisson e·l fol brut e·l feiner?
Q'el mon non es tan folla res
com feing drutz peintenat plaides
1690 e la dompna q'en lui se fia
sera grieu q'al derer s'en ria.
Eu vos en hai dig mon vezaire
e vos fai oimais vostre afaire,
e qant comandares: "Monta(i)tz!",
1695 eu serai del[s] premiers armatz.
Totz francz hom veia la vejansa,
e perda Dieu qi non los lansa
en foc envolz, sebelis vius,
los traitors lausengiers caiti[u]s

fol. 46ᵛ col. 1

col. 2

1665 MS *vaz*   1670 MS *faz*   1683 MS *mas parler*

He considers gossip an honour there
and behaves like the hart which the hunters
and the greyhounds are just catching up with
1665 but departs safely
and can save itself before all,
but it pleases it so much when it hears the dogs
barking that it returns and knows nothing
until it is dead and held by all.
1670 He who approves of foolish gossip behaves in
the same way: he betrays himself and his lady,
for rather should he be of such conduct
that if love attracts his eye so much,
and makes him look at his lady,
1675 he should turn his face away quickly.
A thoughtless facial expression ruins love relationships
and brings condemnation from other people,
and know well that Slander
is like the archer
1680 who draws and wounds with his arrow
the bird whilst it is singing;
in this way the tiresome slanderers
wound joyful lovers
with their tongues, God hate them,
1685 and bring them a living death!
Why do you not teach them, fine lord,
to leave foolish gossip and vanity alone?
For in the whole world there is not so foolish a creature
as a presumptuous, conceited and quarrelsome lover
1690 and the lady who trusts in him
will hardly have cause to be happy about it in the end.
I have told you my opinion
and I will now carry out your business for you,
and when you give the order "Mount up!",
1695 I will be amongst the first armed.
May every honest man see the revenge,
and may anyone be damned, who does not throw them
engulfed into the fire, buried alive,
the treacherous base slanderers

1700 e las traïritz desonradas
don li drut han avolz seudadas,
q'er cujon trobar bona fe
e·l falsa lengua ditz lor be
e van simplas com una monza,
1705 e·l fals cor es plens de mensonza.
Oi, bona gens, fin(s) amador,
tug es mort qi non vos secor.
E vos es plens de gentilesa
e trobas engan et (a)malesa.
1710 E qi pot soffrir la dolor
qe l'uel[s] de bella dompna plor
per manasas e per malditz?
E deves l'autra part l'amictz,
qar sap q'hom la destreing per lui,
1715 totz lo(s) deportz q'el ha s'en fui.
Amors, si aiso non venzatz
totz es vostre prez abaissatz.'
[A]pres Sens ha parlat Zovens.
Molt fon adretz, francs e valens.
1720 Gent li destreis (sor) sas blozas cris
la garlanda de flor de lis
. . . .

THE COURT OF LOVE 135

1700 and the dishonoured treacherous women
from whom lovers have base rewards,
for they now think they have found good faith
and the false tongue praises them
and they go about, innocent as a nun,
1705 but their false heart is full of deception.
Oh, good people, true lovers,
he is completely dead who does not help you.
You are full of nobility
and you find deceit and irritation.
1710 For who can bear the sadness
when the eye of a beautiful lady weeps
on account of threats and slander?
And as for her companion, on the other hand,
because he knows that one torments her because of him,
1715 all the distraction he has disappears.
Love, if you do not avenge this
your worth is entirely abased.'
    After Judgement, Youth spoke.
    He was very just, honest and worthy.
1720 The garland of lilies
nobly held his blond hair,
. . . .

NOTES

❖

1: *seinor*. The subject case is only narrowly the preferred case for the vocative (cf. Jensen, 6–7), so this is not necessarily a plural. For further subject case vocatives in this text, see ll. 838, 881, 954, 1188 (but, for object case vocatives, cf. ll. 101, 377, 879). However, the oral presentation of this text (cf. *auzatz*, l. 5) makes a plural audience more likely.

21–5: This passage is obscure. Constans joins ll. 21–8 together in one sentence, and does not even add his habitual question mark for obscure passages. It would be interesting to know exactly what he made of it. Jones splits the section up into two sentences, but her reasoning (judging by her translation) falls down on several counts. She translates ll. 21–2 as 'For this reason they have made a new love / For a lady of great merit.' Although *de* can mean 'for' (cf. Raynouard, iii. 17), 'they' must presumably refer back to *Malvestat e Putaria* (l. 19), which is illogical. To then account for l. 24 being a relative clause, Jones makes the main verb governed by the *donas qe pulsellas* (l. 23) *fugon* [*sic*] from l. 26, whose subject is clearly *las falsas e·ls fals* (also in l. 26). Grammatically, the only way one can read this passage is to take the *donas qe pulsellas* to be the subject of *han* (l. 21), but who are the *donas qe pulsellas* and what is this *amor / d'una domna de gran valor*? I think, given the opposing gendered discourses of love in this work, that it is a question of making love (/Love?) feminine. Thus either they have made a new concept of love *for* a lady of great merit, or a new personification Love *out of* a lady of great merit (i.e. presenting Love *as* a lady of great merit). See also my Introduction on this point.

27: Hypometric. Constans: *Q[e] a*. PD does give *tant* as an adjective: 'si grand', but as *tant* is more commonly an adverb, there may well be either a past participle (e.g. *a tant [fait] Amors parlament*) or an adjective (e.g. *a tant [fin/gran] Amors parlament*) missing.

28: All other editors read *taing haza*, but this is syntactically very odd. For -*ngh*- as a grapheme for a liquid nasal, see Zufferey, *Recherches*, 262–3.

29: Mahn follows the MS here. Bartsch corrects to *ar aujatz*; Chabaneau to *ora aujatz*. Given that word division is often irregular in this text, it seems simpler to follow Constans in moving the *a* forward. This line is hypermetric, and Constans expunctuates: *com(ent)*.

30: Hypermetric. Constans: *dousa e·l bona*.

NOTES 137

33: Hypometric. The emendation *acorda[da]men*, suggested by Chabaneau, has the advantage of removing the syntactic awkwardness of the sentence. Constans, who had opted for *faz[ia]* in 1881, followed Chabaneau in his revision. Bartsch gives *acordamens*, and then *jutgamens* in l. 34, which presumably he intends as plural oblique forms.

38: *vei*. This is the usual first-person singular form of *vezer*. Although it might sound more elegant if the nightingale were singing on account of the season which *he* sees renewing itself (given *pel*, linking ll. 37 and 38), this kind of abrupt first-person intervention is not uncommon in medieval narrative. Further doubt is created by an unusual morphological feature of this text. There are four occasions where *vei* is definitely used to denote a third-person subject (ll. 136, 373, 1132, 1248), as well as three occasions where it definitely denotes a first-person subject (ll. 364, 741, 760). The usual third-person form, *ve*, also occurs (ll. 133, 139, 291, 1305).

45: *Paors* has two syllables throughout the text. Bartsch gives *Bos Espers, Ancha e Paors* and Mahn *bon esper ancha* ... The MS has *Bonesperancha epaors*.

46: *portent*. Third-person plural forms in *-nt* are gallicisms (see Paul Meyer, 'Les troisièmes personnes du pluriel en provençal', *Romania* 9 (1883), 192–215 (198, 214 and *passim*)). Other instances occur in this text at ll. 69, 376, 1145 and 1622.

50: The MS lesson *idesa* is unattested elsewhere. Raynouard (iii. 553) cites *iderzon* 'buisson', but this seems unlikely in the context. *PSW* (iv. 223) discounts Raynouard's suggestion, calling the word 'sehr fraglich', and cites Chabaneau, who suggests emending it to *ruesa*. Bartsch simply expunctuates the *i*, giving *de sa floria*, but in that case, we must read *floria* as a substantivized past participle, which seems unlikely. This line is hypermetric, and there is a possible internal dittography of *i* [i.e. the last minim of *n*] *des*, so, like Constans, I follow Chabaneau's correction. *ruesa* is to be taken in a collective sense (on which see Jensen, 20, and the note to l. 94, below). On *ruesa*, see the Glossary.

53: Hypometric. Bartsch proposes adding *Car* at the start of the line. Constans in 1881 opted for *mon[ta]*, but in his revision followed Chabaneau's suggestion to add *E* at the start of the line.

54: *envoza*. i.e. *envoia*. This is a gallicism—on which see the Glossary. Bartsch gives *enueja* ('desires'), which is also credible, whilst changing the extent of Amor's agency here.

58: *devant*. The two usual forms in Occitan are *denant* (cf. l. 46) and *davant* (cf. l. 83). *devant*, which also occurs in l. 726, is a gallicism.

61: *chascuna ha*. Initial *h-* does not, as one might expect, always indicate a lack of elision (cf. ll. 83, 428, 489, 542, 1551, 1629).

63: This line is hypometric and has the form of *e* usually only found before a vowel. I follow Chabaneau's suggested correction. An alternative solution, proposed by Bartsch and Constans, is to take the *ez* to contain a

138 NOTES

reflexive pronoun (i.e. *e se*), and to add another *ez* at the start of the line. Although the grapheme *z* does occur in situations where an *s* is orthographically more common, there are no other examples of it serving as a reflexive pronoun in this text. *PSW* (i. 61) lists *braissar*, but as this text is the only instance, he suggests the line should read [*a*]*braissar*, given that the line is hypometric otherwise. Raynouard (ii. 253) cites Old French *braser*, which suggests the *a-* may have been dropped during the *Cort d'Amor*'s transmission in northern France.

65: Hypometric. Constans adds [*E*] at the start of the line. Notice also the parataxis between ll. 65 and 66 (for the omission of *que* in this way, see Jensen, 337–40).

68: Hypometric. Bartsch proposes *auzel*[*et*], whilst Constans prefers [*bel*] *auzel*. *auzel*[*o*] would also be possible.

74: *con d'aur*. This could either be construed 'as if with gold', or 'with gold' (in the latter case taking *d'* to be a partitive article, on which see Jensen, 78–9). I opt for the latter solution as there is no reason why Amor should not be afforded the genuine article.

76: *claus son*. Constans first (1881) went for *clauson*, then (1882), no doubt appreciating the problems inherent in this solution, corrected to *claus an*. He obviously felt unhappy with the notion of two abstractions *being* keys, but this type of emblematic allegory is extremely common in medieval texts.

86: *le*. As this is in an oblique case, we would expect the form *lo*. The same phenomenon occurs in ll. 369, 883 and 1101. Jensen records an accusative *le* in 'quelques chartes toulousaines' (60), but more likely here is that this is another gallicism, the standard masculine oblique singular form in Old French being *le*.

88: Hypometric. *cant qe* as an indefinite pronoun is rare in Occitan (Jensen, 178).

93–4: For *menudet*, PD gives an adjective, 'tout petit', and an adverb, 'de façon serrée'. As a lily is not particularly tiny, I have opted for the second of these. In either case, the singular verb form *nais* (l. 94) indicates that one must correct *flor*(*s*) and understand the resulting singular lily in a collective sense (on which see Jensen, 20): 'the fountain is crowned with a lily, and lilies grow all over the meadow'.

97: Although the orthography of *enaissi* clearly suggests three syllables, the metre demands only two, which raises the question of why an orthography like *aisi* was not preferred. See my Editorial Principles on this point. Constans (1882), perhaps deciding that the middle syllable of *enaissi* could be clipped in pronunciation, also retains the full form, after having expunctuated *en* in 1881.

98: Mahn has *ad estreigner*. Despite the apparent awkwardness, *ha a* must be elided.

107–8: As it stands in the MS, l. 108 can either mean 'the lion killed the ant' or 'the ant killed the lions'. Although I hesitate to emend a perfectly correct lesson, I feel it is justifiable on a number of counts. Firstly, the use of inflectional -s is far from regular in this text. Other instances of singular oblique nouns incorrectly taking -s occur at ll. 909 and 1261. Secondly, 'the ant kills the lions' can be rejected, both because only one lion is mentioned in l. 115, and because fables tend to pair individual animals. Thirdly, 'the lion kills the ant', given the links made between the animals and the knave and the lady in ll. 115–16, would associate the lady with an insect and the knave with the king of the beasts. It seems much more reasonable to imagine a fable where the noble lion is brought to grief through the treachery of a lowly ant. This would certainly fit the standard pattern of a diminutive animal overcoming a great one in the fable tradition (cf. 'The Gnat and the Lion', no. 188 in Aesop's *Fables* (trans. Olivia and Robert Temple, Penguin Classics, 1998)). Unfortunately, no fable of specifically an ant and a lion has been traced. Previous scholarship has also failed to establish the exact reference to, or the identity of, Iohanitz. Johannitius was the name by which the Latin West knew the eighth-century physician and translator Husayn-ibn-Ishak. Amongst other things, he translated the *Oneirocritica* of Artemidorus, a second-century handbook for the interpretation of dreams. In ch. 24 of the first book of the *Oneirocritica*, Artemidorus speaks of dreams involving ears (references are to the translation by Robert J. White, *The Interpretation of Dreams: 'Oneirocritica' by Artemidorus* (Park Ridge: Noyes, 1975), 28): 'To dream that ants are entering one's ears is auspicious only for sophists. For the ants are like young men who attend courses [to listen to teachers]. But for other men, the dream prophesies death. For ants are children of the earth and they go down into the earth. [. . .] If a man dreams that he has the ears of a lion, wolf, leopard, or of any other wild beast, it signifies a plot against him that will arise from slander.' Although there is no direct reference to an ant killing lions here, the association of ants with garrulousness and death, and the lion with the victims of slander, fits our context. Given the many points of contact between the *Cort d'Amor* and the *De Amore* of Andreas Capellanus, it is interesting to note that the latter also refers to Johannitius. In iii. 58, Andreas writes: 'Johannicius says that sleep gives rest to the animal powers and intensifies the sexual ones, so loss of sleep connotes precisely the wearying of our animal powers and the weakening of our sexual ones.' This citation has not been traced (see the note in Walsh's edition, p. 305, from which I quote), nor is it from the *Oneirocriticon*, but the theme of sleep and dreaming does give it some kind of link with the *Oneirocriticon*. Perhaps both our author and Andreas were familiar with a compendium of ideas on dreams with which the name of Johannitius was associated. Unfortunately this theory remains speculative, but archival work may shed further light on the issue.

140 NOTES

111: *us.* This functions as a numeral here (cf. Jensen, 73–4).

109–14: The syntax is a little convoluted here, but the complaint of Amor is basically that Joi makes lovers joyful whether or not they are discreet, and that the lady takes the blame for it.

128: *son cors cobrir:* literally, 'to be discreet with regard to himself' (for *son cors* as an emphatic for 'him', see Jensen, 88), although there may also be an intended pun with the even more literal reading 'to cover his body'—the imperative to be discreet reduces the lover's potential for naked dalliance.

136: *ve(i).* See note to l. 38.

140: *es pesz qu'a morta.* Mahn has *espez qua morta* and Bartsch *espes qu'a morta.* Presumably from *espesar,* 'to destroy'? The implication of this syntactically dense passage is that the churl sees a courtly lover approaching and so shuts the door to his house and beats his wife because he suspects her of infidelity. The simile is clarified by the lover carrying a lure and a trap, but although the lover is presumably interested in trapping the churl's wife, it is the churl himself who is compared to the bird which flees a trap.

152: Constans adds *e* between *viulas* and *dansas. viulas* normally has just two syllables, but *PSW* (viii. 790), cites another example of it being trisyllabic, in *Daurel et Beton* (l. 85). It is definitely trisyllabic when it recurs in this text at l. 890, where it is at the rhyme.

154: *seigna.* Constans corrects to *seigua,* following Chabaneau's suggestions of *segua* (hunt down). As Constans points out, *i* before a liquid nasal is a common feature of this text (cf. ll. 353, 370 etc.).

161: *la fasse(i)tz.* Bartsch gives *fazetz.* Constans keeps *laffasseitz,* despite Chabaneau's proposed correction to *la fasetz.* The *i* seems superfluous in any case, but it remains to decide whether to remove an *s,* to give a rare imperative form found in *Girart de Roussillon* (see Anglade, 333), or to change the *e* to an *a* to give a jussive subjunctive. Since *s* is doubled elsewhere in this text without changing the phonetic effect (cf. *gaiessa* in l. 145, which rhymes with *pesa,* l. 146), I have in fact merely expunctuated the *i.*

161–4: It is interesting that the girl should go to her lover, not vice versa. This reversal of the typical *alba* situation is perhaps motivated by the issues of male and female attitudes towards love at play throughout the text.

166: *terre* is a gallicism. Occurring at the rhyme, it is less likely that this is merely a scribal contribution. If *terre* were emended to *terra, enqerre* would have to become *enqerra,* and *a* (l. 165) become *qe.*

168: The syntax seems inordinately convoluted and inelegant here. Jones reads *enuei* as *envei,* but this form is unattested and her translation of this line 'I will certainly make you do what you desire' is contrary to the context. The remark that the lover is 'not afraid of anything' (l. 169) when he sets about serving his lady implies that he has not received a favourable response to his initial declaration of love. Chabaneau proposes correcting

NOTES 141

to *eu be farai con eu vei / ton enuei*, the first of which does not seem to make any sense in the context, and the second of which does not significantly ease the syntax. Constans chooses to retain the MS lesson, without signalling any difficulty here.

172: Hypometric. Constans adds *pueis* [*el*] *la*. Chabaneau suggests either *pueis* [*vos*] or [*e*] *pueis*. Bartsch gives *lo fatz*, but this change is quite unnecessary.

174: *paraie* rhymes with *lignatje* (l. 173).

178: *ardi*[*da*]*ment*. Not only is this line hypometric, but the syntax also requires something extra. Bartsch and Constans prefer [*ab*] *ardiment*.

182: Hypometric in the MS. Constans emends *dir*[*e*], but the rhetoric demands [*totz*]. Amor *can* say what good things he has from Corteszia—he goes on to do so (ll. 185–94). The point is that he can't possibly relate *all* the good things he has from her.

196: Chabaneau claims there must be at least two lines missing following this verse. Certainly the sudden appearance of an implicit third-person subject in l. 197 is abrupt. Constans runs ll. 195–200 into one long sentence, and does not comment on any difficulty.

199: *comensa la pregar*. *Comensar* + infinitive is perfectly well attested (*PSW*, i. 295; cf. Raynouard, ii. 446), but Constans prefers *commens'a la pregar* [*sic*].

204: *ben* could be either an adverb or a noun. In the latter case, the lover's hopes take on a more tangible goal. No doubt a pun is intended.

206: Constans gives *a*[*l*] *premier*, and points to the similarity with the start of l. 197. *PSW* (vi. 556) corrects Constans and cites a further example of *a premier*.

211: Constans has *plens es*, and follows Chabaneau's correction of *vos* to *vas* in l. 212, which would give 'you are full of deceit towards lovers, which is why . . .', which seems to me an unlikely reproach for the lady to make in this situation. *es* is attributed as a second-person plural form (for the more common *etz*), but then there would be a redundant -*s* on *plens*. I follow Levy's proposed correction, although *ses* is a very rare alternative to *etz* (Anglade, 314).

213–14: *aison*. *aiso* (from *ecce hoc*) should not, etymologically, have an -*n*, and this is no doubt a case of assimilation. *boton* (l. 214) does have a final unstable -*n*, and so rhymes with *aiso* (cf. ll. 549–50).

215: *el*. This is most unusually used as a third-person singular feminine form here and at ll. 755, 1009, 1132 and possibly l. 964 (see note to that line). This is a gallicism.

220: Hypometric. Constans misreads *Qe el*.

229: *mandetz*. Constans corrects to *mandes*, Chabaneau suggests *mandei*. This is evidently by analogy with the second-person forms in ll. 233–6. I think, however, that the poet uses the two different second-person forms deliberately to make the outlines of this interior dialogue more distinct. The sample lover is split into two, the first bemoaning his fate pathetically and using the polite plural form to address the second, who is more vituperative in his language and addresses the first using the more familiar singular form. Only the first uses first-person forms. From l. 240 onwards, it becomes difficult to identify two distinct voices, so I have not used speech marks to delineate the two 'speakers'.

232: *se tener a* is usually followed by an adjective and means 'to consider oneself' (Jensen, 314). Here the context indicates that it is a question of the lady considering (*tener a*) the speaker to be proud, so *se* must be understood as a dative: 'to herself', i.e. 'inwardly'.

237: *sa[be]z*. Hypometric in the MS. Constans adds a syllable *q'e[la]*, whilst keeping *saz*. He presumably forgets the convention of standardizing to *-i* in final position after a vowel, as otherwise it is difficult to see what form he does envisage *saz* to constitute. It is not difficult to imagine why a scribe would write a first-person form (final *-z* being common for *-i* throughout the text), given the following *m'*. This passage is dense on account of the interior dialogue carried out by the sample fearful lover, with the poet seemingly trying to keep the two sides of that dialogue clear by alternating *-tz* and *-s* forms. Here I think we have an instance of the former, but I have omitted the *t* by analogy with ll. 662 and 1476.

247–8: Constans punctuates *Aici vos dic: 'On nos estem, / Ren non ama om qe non tem.'*

251: *proesa*. Jones misreads as *pesa* here and in l. 255. She correctly reads *pesa* in l. 457, but translates as 'prowess' in all cases anyway.

255: MS *noncell*. The second *n* here, as at l. 257, may be the result of an incorrectly expanded abbreviation. The verb is thus a clipped form of *escelar*, 'to instruct'.

256: Hypometric as it stands in the MS. *cobetsa* seems to be an orthographical mistake, as it does not rhyme with *proesa* (l. 255), and the usual form elsewhere in the MS is *cobezesa* (cf. ll. 742, 841, 868). *cobeesa* also exists (ll. 263, 1596), but the two adjacent *es* are not elided. Constans corrects *orba* to *orda* (?).

257: MS *nincell*. See note to l. 255.

272: Jones capitalizes *Joy* [*sic*] and makes it the subject of *dara* in l. 271.

285: Hypometric. Constans adds: *es [ben] la*.

292: Chabaneau proposes *aiatz talant*.

293–4: *locs* (l. 293) is a nominative singular, *iocs* (l. 294) an accusative plural, which is why I have emended *vostre[s]*. Constans expunctuates the final *s* in each line, but this makes l. 293 ungrammatical. He was presumably uncomfortable with *iocs* being plural.

300: *doin*. This is a gallicism.

303: My emendation solves two problems. Firstly, there is no verb in ll. 303–4 and, *son bel amic* (l. 304) being an oblique case, they cannot simply be in apposition to *fina druda* (l. 301). Secondly, *res* (l. 303), being a subject form, cannot be in apposition to *son bel amic*. To maintain correct scansion, *re a* must be elided. Levy proposes a similar solution: *E ce* (=*se*) *la ren qi plus li platz, / Son bel amic* [*a*] *entrels bratz*...?

308: *enueia*. Constans and Jones read *enveja/enveia*. This seems highly unlikely given the lover's response in l. 309.

315: *ni Soredamors*. Constans does not get the reference and gives *no saup re d'amors*, doubting Chabaneau's suggestion that it might be the name of a character from a romance. Unlike the two couples cited in ll. 316–17, Gauvain and Soredamors are not lovers, but brother and sister in Chrétien's *Cligès*. This would suggest that the author of our text was not thoroughly familiar with the story as told by his northern colleague.

325: Jones reads [D]*rudaria, vos es Dons Pres* and translates '*Drudaria*, you and Lord Merit'.

327: *dez*. Constans corrects to *dui*, despite Levy's explanation that it refers to the ten previously addressed personifications from Joi to Dousa Compaina. If Constans takes *dui* to refer to Drudaria and Pretz, who does he think is being addressed at this point?

330: This line is hypometric once the irregular *t* has been expunged. Given that there are already a *la* and a *lo* in this line, it is not difficult to understand how the scribe could have missed another *lo* just before the *la*. As if to prove this point, Constans does the opposite and marks the additional *lo* without noticing (or at least without marking) its absence in the MS.

331: Hypometric. Constans adds *hajon* [*nul*] *be*. In fact the whole passage seems corrupt, given that l. 333 is hypermetric. Possible dittographies between ll. 331 and 332 (*aion*), and between ll. 332 and 333 (*domnas*), may be at the root of the problem. See also note to l. 333.

333: Hypermetric. Constans (1881) expunctuated *si* but in his 1882 revision chose to expunctuate the -*on* of *prenon* instead. The subject of this singular verb form he presumably takes to be the prisoner referred to in ll. 328–30, but in this case one wonders what the subject of the plural *haion* in l. 332 is. He ignores Chabaneau's suggested alterations: correcting *prenon* to *son*, whilst expunctuating the final -*n* on *n'aion* in l. 332, taking *domnas* in l. 332 to be dative. Chabaneau does not, however, propose correcting the *haion* in l. 331 so the plural/singular problem remains as with Constans. Perhaps the simplest solution is to accept the hypermetricity of l. 333 as authorial.

335–6: Levy suggests expunctuating the final -*s* on these two lines, but this seems slightly awkward given the plural possessive adjective *lur* and plural pronoun *lor*.

345: *hac s'a gran*. Bartsch gives *ac a gran*, but *s* (*so*) is governed by *comandat* (l. 346).

355: Hypermetric. Bartsch corrects *domnas qu'elas son*; Constans prefers *donnas coma son*.

144 NOTES

359: *soltiment*. i.e. *sotilment*. This is a gallicism.
361: *a gardar*. Mahn misreads *agardar*, Bartsch changes to *agradar*, Jones misreads *e gardar*.
362: *dei'ostar*. Bartsch proposes correcting to *deu ostar*; following Chabaneau, I read the MS lesson as a contraction of *deia ostar*.
365: *qe·m*. In the MS this is *q̄ē*. Constans and Jones prefer to expand to *qen*.
367: *sab*. Levy needlessly suggests correcting to *sai*.
369: *le*. See note to l. 86.
373: *ve(i)*. See note to l. 38.
375: *puis*. This is a gallicism (for *pus*) which also occurs in ll. 652, 715 and 1560.
376: *font*. See note to l. 46.
380: Hypometric. Constans: *que orgueill*.
381: *ai·n*. All other editors have read this as *am*, owing to the somewhat careless use of minims in the MS. Constans is the only one to notice a problem with such a form here, and corrects by expunctuating the *m*.
383: *ben*. Constans and Jones misread as *breu*.
384: *breuiar*. Constans gives *breviar*, but *PSW* (i. 165) rejects this form.
389: Jones gives *terza es mesura*, remarking that 'the manuscript does not show *si*', as Constans had read. *Pace* Jones, the MS does read *terza si es mesura*.
390: *per*. This could either be 'on account of' or 'amongst' (cf. Raynouard, iv. 503–4). The former tends to highlight the agency of the *g[e]nt tafura*, and so is rather out of place in a definition of the qualities of *fin'amor* which Corteszia is outlining here.
398: Hypermetric. Constans: *e·ls comunals* (i.e. 'the base men' ?). The second *las* could be expunctuated altogether to reduce the syllable count without changing the gender.
399: There is a possible dittography of *lor* within the line, as it is not clear to whom the first *lor* refers. Constans opts for a more substantial correction: *Que lor sembels(?) et lor(s) amors*; Chabaneau is more ingenious with *que lor fe menten, lor amors(?)*.
401: *devem*. Constans misreads *deven*. Levy suggests correcting *aqellas* to *aquella*, presumably taking it to refer to *la falsa via bastarsa* (l. 395), which makes sense if the women in ll. 397–8 are simply an enumeration of *la gent* in l. 396. Although this is quite plausible, it is also possible that the women are in apposition to *la falsa via bastarsa*: i.e. 'we shouldn't talk about the false, illegitimate way . . . *or* the women of ill-repute . . .'. This distinction is grammatical rather than semantic inasmuch as the women in question clearly are being identified with *la gent*. The late appearance of the main verb in l. 401, combined with the two sub-clauses, makes this long sentence a little difficult to construe. We must take ll. 395–400 to be oblique and thus governed by *d'* in l. 401.

403: *fait d'Amor*. Does this mean that Corteszia has merely been iterating a judgement (previously) made by Amor? Or that she has made the judgement *for* Amor (cf. note to l. 22)? Or that her judgement is made of love (to be distinguished from Love)? Constans seems to opt for the last of these three as he does not capitalize *amor* here. Jones gives *fait d'Amor*, 'made by Love'.

409: *han*. Bartsch gives *lian*.

417: *La Cortesa d'Amor*. Bartsch suggests correcting to *Na Cortezia d'Amor*. Jones reads *La* as an adverb of place, thus translating the line 'There Courtesy takes it from Love'. On the question of Cortesa d'Amor as a separate figure, see my Introduction.

432: *aduiszon*. Constans reads as *adviszon*, but this makes poor sense in this context.

437: *trobares*. *-s*, instead of *-tz*, in the second person plural is common from the first half of the thirteenth century, see Anglade, 270.

440: The sense here clearly demands the elimination of the negative. This may be the miscopying of a former abbreviation.

444: *pensa*. Levy corrects to *pesa*, as it clearly has to rhyme with *felnesa* (l. 443). Another example of this occurs in ll. 507–8, where *mesa* rhymes with *pensa*. For Latin *-ns-* assimilated to *-ss-*, see Anglade, 186–7. Cf. *pessa* in l. 1069.

453: *fazia*. i.e. *faria*. Clearly a conditional form is required, although Bartsch alone corrects to *faria*. On *z* for *r* in this MS, see also note to l. 843.

460: This is the only example in this text of final *-z* for *-i* after a consonant. See also Glossary for *manti*.

461: It is easy to see why the scribe might have written *pus*, as it occurs in ll. 459 and 460, but the sense here precludes a comparative. This line is hypometric. Constans adds: *devenc [tan] pus*.

463: *vous*. This is a gallicism. Cf. l. 469.

466: *soplei ab*. Constans reads *soplei'ab*, but *soplei* is a jussive subjunctive like *digua* in l. 467.

467–8: As Constans remarks, these two lines seem to be inverted. Like Constans, however, I maintain the MS order because it is syntactically possible, even if inelegant.

469: *vous*. This is a gallicism. Cf. l. 463.

477: Hypometric. Constans apparently misreads *proesa* for *pesa*, which is probably simply a case of the scribe missing the horizontal bar over the *p*.

480: *ve(z)*. Constans maintains *vez*, but only a third-person form makes sense here. This is perhaps another example of *vei* being used as a third-person form (see note to l. 38).

489: *Qe hai* must be elided for correct scansion. See also note to l. 61.

496: *aimon*. This is a gallicism.

505: Bartsch gives *respon de cauzida*; Constans and Jones give *responda causida*. (Jones translates *causida* as 'carefully'.)

508: *pensa.* See note to l. 444. Constans expunctuates the *n*, although he did not in l. 444; he also gives *al re* instead of *alre.*

510: *s'ieu so dic.* Constans gives *sieus o dic*, although given that he does not use the enclitic dot, it is hard to tell exactly how he construed *sieus*. Presumably he had in mind the version favoured by Jones: *si eu·s o dic*. The addition of the second-person pronoun ·*s* changes the meaning very little, and *si eu·s* must be elided to maintain proper scansion.

513: *vos es.* Bartsch suggests *no·us esjauszit*, but the context makes it clear that the problem is maintaining men's interest *after* they have had their way, not before.

518: *el mez.* Given the ambivalence of *z*, this could be either *el mes*, 'within the month', or *el mei*, 'in the meantime'.

526: On *i* as a contraction of *li*, see Jensen, 294–5.

528: *esdeve.* Constans and Jones both misread *el deve.*

536: *que·l.* Constans expunctuates the *l.*

539: Chabaneau suggests correcting to *aquest ben covinent?*

540: Constans misreads *sor.*

550: *bell e.* Constans corrects to *bella*. The rhyming of *faissons* with *ioios* (l. 549) shows the extent of final unstable -*n* in Occitan.

553: *e acuella.* Constans misreads *cacuella*, then (1881) corrects to *qels acuella*. Following Levy's suggestion, he later (1882) corrects to *els acuella*. They are evidently anxious about the lack of a direct object for *acuella*. In fact, the direct object is clearly *messages* (l. 551), which is however introduced by *als*, because the verbs in l. 552 take indirect objects. Perhaps *Als* in l. 551 should be emended to *E·ls* (which as a general oblique could refer to direct or indirect objects) or perhaps the author (or a scribe) felt that the direct object was clear enough from context and did not need to be grammatically shown.

560: Hypermetric. *femina* is probably a contribution from the Italian scribe, and Constans emends to *femna*. Occitan did have a trisyllabic form, *femena* (cf. l. 399, and Raynouard, iii. 302).

564: The MS's *lausimet* is not attested, although see *PSW* (iv. 346) for a discussion of *lauzimanier* in Giraut de Bornelh.

569: *s'en blasma.* Chabaneau, followed by Constans (1882), suggests *l'en blasma*, but *se blasmar* 'se plaindre' (*PD*, 48) is perfectly acceptable.

570: Hypometric. Constans: *al[tre]tant.*

574: The word division in the MS gives a surprising preterite form (*volc*) and an obscure end to the line. The verb is *autar*, 'plaire' (*PD*, 34). See also *PSW*, i. 104.

575: *an soven.* Constans and Jones give *anso ven*, but *ven*, unlike *an*, is not a jussive subjunctive.

578: Hypometric. Constans: *embras[se].*

595: Hypermetric. The simplest way to correct would be to expunctuate *la*. Constans misreads (?) *garda quel plu(s)ma.*

601: Hypermetric. Constans: *Que quil baisza.*

NOTES   147

602: Hypometric. Constans: *q'haja l[o] cors.*
609: *loing.* This is a gallicism not just in form but also in meaning: 'for a long time'.
614: *gai[a] re.* Constans: *g[au]dire.*
623: *gars.* Constans corrects: *gart.*
626: Chabaneau, followed by Constans (1882), corrects to *si [lo] cors consen el coindia*; Levy proposes *si [sos] cors consen et coindia*. It is difficult to make either of these fit with what precedes and follows this line. More likely is a scribal error, misreading an abbreviation sign *cor'* (?). *Coindia*, throughout the text, is trisyllabic.
628: This line seems to be very corrupt. I can do no better than adopt Chabaneau's elegant solution.
645: Hypometric. Constans adds *E* at the start of the line, and corrects to *triche ges* to provide a jussive subjunctive.
651: Hypometric. Constans, following Chabaneau, corrects *On plus lav[ar] om lai fezes*, albeit marking his uncertainty with a question mark. Presumably they did not recognize *laisezes* as an imperfect subjunctive from *laizar* ('souiller', *PD*, 221). The extra syllable could be provided by inserting *ja* between *la* and *non*; indeed following *la*, it is not difficult to imagine how a scribe might have skipped over it.
652: *puis.* This is a gallicism.
655: *d[a]urar.* The MS lesson is not impossible: 'nor, any more than one can strengthen [*durar*] tin', as tin is only used for coating or in alloys. *cobrar* (l. 656), however, suggests that 'gild' is necessary for the metaphor.
661: *plan agardat.* Constans and Jones give *plana gardat*, but the adjective needs to agree with *ill cabeill* (l. 657). The meaning seems to be, literally, 'let her hair be considered smooth'.
662: *e volt.* Constans unnecessarily emends to *ab volt*, not seeing *volt* as a past participle.
675: Hypermetric. Constans expunctuates: *port(e)*. Final *-e* is optional on singular subjunctive forms.
690: *e an ab.* Constans misreads the first letter, which leads him to emend: *Can[t] [es] ab*.
695: *an[s] sia.* If we read *ans ia coindamen* this line is hypometric.
702: Chabaneau suggests a lacuna after this line. Certainly the switch from personal hygiene to social behaviour is abrupt, but not totally out of the question either.
703: Hypermetric. Constans expunctuates *tot*.
714: This line is hypermetric if the last syllable of *blasme(t)* and the *i* are not elided. *blasmet* is not attested as a form, so I have expunctuated the *t*. Perhaps the original was *blasmat* and the *i* mistakenly added later? See note to l. 715. Constans misreads *blasme ei*, and simply expunctuates an *e*. Jones misreads *blasme n'hai*.

715: [*un*]. Hypometric. The fact that *i* in l. 714 is potentially superfluous suggests that an *.i.* (an abbreviation for *un*) could have been transposed forward a line by the scribe. Constans misreads and corrects: *tot entr[es]ait*. *puis* is a gallicism.

716: Constans gives *mals esma, part e fait* and admits that he does not understand this line.

722: *n'es ges*. The MS lesson would seem to be a mistake of abbreviation, for *non ges* would leave us without a verb in l. 722, nor can we simply understand *seria* from l. 721 because the conditional mode would not fit l. 722.

723: *sospe*. *l* for *s* is an easy scribal error. If we were to accept *los pe*, the closed *e* would not rhyme with the open *e* of *merce* (l. 724), the only troubadour to rhyme open and closed *e*s being the Italian Bartolomeo Zorzi (cf. Paul Meyer, 'L'imparfait du subjonctif en *es*', *Romania* 8 (1879), 155–62). On the hapax *sospe*, see the Glossary. The line thus construes: 'but let a man (*on*) let (*lais*) suspicion pass away (*anar*) from them (*lor*)'.

724: *venia lur*. *venia* is a subjunctive form of *venir*, the *i* indicating a liquid *n* in place of the more common *h* or *g*. *lur* is a rare plural dative form (Anglade, 248).

729: *vista*. On the gender of Merce, see my Introduction.

730: *non sapcha hom*. Constans misreads the last word as *bon*, which no doubt leads Chabaneau to correct *non* to *no·l*.

750: *e·l bailla*. Constans emends to *e·ls bailla*, which would give 'he who promises and gives money' (in fact, Constans needlessly swaps *los* with *lor* in l. 751). The MS lesson *e·l bailla* (= *e li bailla*), giving 'he who promises money and power', may seem less likely, given that the following lines insist on money alone, but I hesitate from correcting a perfectly correct MS version.

755: *el* 'she'. See note to l. 215.

768: *autre*. Constans does not correct here, but surely a masculine form is required.

771: *s'enaisi i clama*. Constans follows Chabaneau's correction to *s'enaisi·l clama*.

785: *garen*. Constans corrects to *ganre*, i.e. 'deprive them of much of their advantage'.

786: *qe quant om dis* ... The main clause here is clumsily put at the end of this long speech, in l. 803.

799: *coiton*. Jones misreads *coiron* and translates 'torment'.

801: Hypermetric. Constans, following Chabaneau, corrects *feses* to *fos*. He then ends the lover's apostrophe of his eyes at the end of l. 802, giving '"Eyes, luckily was I ever born, for you have cried on account of my lady." How is she worth less, if she answers nobly?'. Constans forgets that he had opened the speech of the lover with a conditional clause in l. 786 and thus

the speech is never finished and the conditional clause never resolved. Line 801 could be reduced to eight syllables simply by expunctuating *anc*.
804: *merceira*. Constans expunctuates the *r*. Admittedly the presence of a future between two presents (ll. 803 and 805) upsets our sense of sequence of tenses. It may be intended to convey a sense of habit (cf. Jensen, 244).
805: *sai*. Jones misreads *fai*.
806: *ço*. Cedillas do occur on three occasions in the text, in ll. 738, 1023 and 1590: quite unnecessarily (before an *e*) in the last two of these occasions.
809: *haurai*. Constans expunctuates the *i*, so that it is the lover who has preserved his own worth, rather than Amor having preserved it for him.
816: Hypometric. It is easy to see how a scribe could have missed *es* as it is also the start of the next word. Constans also corrects *q'ar* to *que*, which simplifies the syntax.
821: Hypermetric. Constans expunctuates the third syllable of *cobe(ze)sas*, but I think that a dittography of the sequence *on vos* in l. 822 is a more readily explicable error and so perhaps *vos* should be expunctuated.
823: *a'tzinadas* (= *a aizinadas*) 'has dealt with'. Constans follows Chabaneau's correction *a zujadas* 'has judged'.
825: *er getat*. Constans misreads *Ez*, and Chabaneau then ingeniously proposes that *ez* = *ei* (from *habeo*). I think we must understand *a* from l. 823.
843: *bruiz*. I.e. *bruir*. Suchier ('Il canzoniere', 50) remarks that *z* for *r* is a common feature of the whole MS. Cf. also l. 453.
847: Hypermetric. Constans expunctuates *a*.
858: *er'iamais*. Constans gives *er jamais*, which is a future. Presumably he understood 'there never will be such a fine court [again]'.
867–8: The *d* in *aunida* (l. 867) was clearly pronounced very softly, to rhyme with *cria* (l. 868). Compare *mercaanda* (for *mercadanda*) in l. 828.
881: *la[u] vostra gran merces*. Constans does not correct here. *la vostra gran merces*, being oblique, makes perfectly good sense: 'thanks to your great mercy'. This, however, would leave us without a main verb for the sentence. Constans admittedly punctuates differently, placing a semicolon at the end of l. 880, but *de. . .del[s]. . .* prevent *l'onor* and *bes* (l. 882) being taken in apposition to *ioi* (l. 880). Cf. the examples in Raynouard (iv. 207–8) and *PSW* (v. 229–30).
883: *le[s] premiers*. The definite article is a gallicism (see note to l. 86). Constans emends to *lo premier*, but the past participle *aiutz* would also suggest a plural direct object.
884: *es*. Levy suggests correcting to *son*, but a singular verb form serving two singular subjects is quite common: see Jensen, 208–9.
886: *sa*. Jones follows the lesson of the MS and translates 'their', but there is no evidence that the singular possessive can indicate plural possessors in this way. In discussing this passage, O. Dammann, *Die allegorische Canzone*

des Guirant de Calanso 'A lieis cui am de cor e de saber' und ihre Deutung (Breslau: Koebner, 1891), 86 & n., corrects to *lor*. One can understand the impulse to do so, as it seems awkward to take the possessor of *sa* to be only one of Rire and Deport, with whom Na Coindia is linked by the fact that she enters with them. Although it may seem slightly inelegant to take the possessive to be governed by *Fin'Amor* in the sub-clause, that is the only solution without doing violence to the MS lesson. The aristocratic title, *Na*, also supports the idea that she is related to noble Amor rather than the jongleurs Rire and Deport, although her activity, dancing with a cymbal (l. 888), is more appropriate for a *joglaressa* than for a noblewoman.

890: *viola*. See note to l. 152.

896: *son cap mogut*. The implication seems to be that Amor adjudicates between the competing claims of Ris, Deport and Na Coindia to be heard first, giving a nod to indicate that Ris is favoured. *por* (for *per*) is a gallicism (cf. l. 1500).

898–902: Constans puts these lines in quotation marks, but *el* (l. 899) must refer to Amor even if, at a stretch, we can imagine the rest of this passage being what Amor said to his seneschal.

903: Probably only one line has been omitted by the scribe here.

906: *de lin Iutas*. Having misread *de linvitas* (1881), Constans corrects to *de lur viltas* (1882), attributing the suggestion to Chabaneau. In fact, Chabaneau rightly suggests *del lin Judas*, which indicates that he revised the corrections he had communicated privately to Constans before publishing them.

909: Hypermetric. Perhaps Constans takes *traïdor* to have only two syllables as he does not correct. *per* could be expunctuated, giving the sense 'condemn the treacherous slanderer'.

918–19: These two lines involve a logical leap. The middle term must be understood from ll. 912–13: as slanderers have brought about the end of their affair, the lady can no longer be accused of anything and the lover's life is no longer worth living .

921: *se lla*. Chabaneau suggests *sella* (= *sen la* = *sine illa*), but this ignores the fact that *cara* must be the subject of *se laissa* (l. 923). Constans prints *sella*, but takes it to be *se la*.

924: *faita*. Constans corrects: *fait o*. There seems to be no obvious reason why this participle should be feminine, if it is not simply a scribal error. Past participles frequently do not agree with their direct objects (Jensen, 232), but the default form is always masculine. There is another example of an inexplicable feminine past participle in l. 1195.

925: *damnia*. This is probably just a case of sloppy minims. This line is hypermetric unless *-ia* is pronounced as one syllable.

927: Constans takes this line to be hypometric and emends: *Que [ja] non*. *puesca* can be trisyllabic (cf. Anglade, 340 n. 2), although it would seem to have only two syllables in ll. 1191 and 1206.

NOTES   151

934: *soleals*. Constans expunctuates the *a*. See Glossary.
941: *nes*. This is a gallicism, the usual Occitan form being *neis*.
943: Hypometric. Constans corrects *dorm*[*i*]. A support vowel (whether etymological or not) is common in verbs with a consonant cluster at the end of the stem (cf. Anglade, 269 and 284), though less likely when the verb is followed by a vowel, as here (*ez*). Alternatively, a horizontal bar may have been inadvertently left off the *q* at the start of the line (i.e. *q*[*e*] *eu*).
948: *e cug q'ades*. There is a possible dittography here from l. 946.
950: *ricedar*. See Glossary. Constans follows Chabaneau's emendation to *ric e clar*.
952: *emdeven*. Constans, following Chabaneau, feels it necessary to correct to *m'endeven*.
956: *do<u>us</u>*. The scribe may well have misread a *u* as an *n* in a previous manuscript. This is not hard to believe if the previous scribe was equally careless with minims.
963: *venduda*. Constans follows Chabaneau's emendation to *vencuda*.
964: *el*. This is used as a feminine pronoun elsewhere in this text (see note to l. 215). Here it makes sense as either 'he' or 'she'. I have opted for the latter solution.
967: *aucire*. On the passive use of infinitives, see Jensen, 217–18.
974: *penren*. *-n* instead of *-m* for the first person plural is rare (Anglade, 270). See also l. 1213.
988–9: *Marcos ... Salamos*. A reference to *Les Dits de Marcoul et de Salomon*, a collection of proverbs in which a sentence from Solomon would be replied to by Marcoul with a popular and usually licentious proverb. Constans notes that the order is reversed here (in that Marcoul is mentioned first), but the implication is simply that despite the base and foolish nature of slanderers, the true lover should mind that his speech remain wise.
994: *cera·n dan*. Constans corrects this to *feran dan*. Presumably 'make a gift'?
995: Hypometric. Constans: *Ans* [*tot*] *lur*.
999: *los*. Constans emends to *lo*, but I think 'them' is the lover *and* his lady (cf. ll. 1000–5). Constans, indeed, further emends *ill* (l. 1003) to *el* (following Chabaneau) to eradicate the issue.
1004: Constans, following Chabaneau, switches the *b* on *Ab* (l. 1004) onto *a* (l. 1005), which would slightly change the meaning: 'he [see note to l. 999] has such a gift that he cares not with what he hides his sincere joy/if he also hides his sincere joy'.
1008: Hypometric. Constans and Chabaneau add *et* instead, i.e. 'her noble and honoured person', and deal with the lack of verb by joining this line syntactically to the following lines.
1009: *el*, 'she'. See note to l. 215.
1011: Hypometric. Constans and Chabaneau: [*E*] *fait tan* . . .

1012: *coves*. i.e. *convens*, 'promises'. For the assimilation of *nv* to *v*, see Anglade, 187.
1017: Hypometric. Constans: *Mangas [e] cordos*.
1018: Hypermetric. Constans: *E si·l mostra. puei* is a gallicism.
1022: *luei*. This is a gallicism.
1025: Hypometric. Constans: *Antz [li] deu*.
1034: *fai*. Chabaneau, followed by Constans, emends to *sai*. Although a dittography of *fai* (cf. ll. 1035 and 1036) is possible, I do not see that their correction is an improvement.
1037: Constans corrects and punctuates this line *Ni autra qi ço, sapcha, s'i fia*. Presumably he takes the subject of *sapcha* to be the fickle lover.
1038: *e ll'apella*. Constans: *ell'apella son amador*.
1045: *zinnosa*. i.e. *ginhosa*.
1055: Hypermetric. Constans expunctuates *ill*.
1058: Hypermetric. Constans expunctuates all of *son*.
1059: Hypermetric. Constans expunctuates *fin*. Alternatively, this line could be taken as the start of a new sentence, and *e* removed from the start of the line.
1061: *deporton*. As this is a first-person plural form, this is a gallicism.
1067: Hypermetric. Constans expunctuates *lo*. There is possibly just one line missing after this one, as Coindia seems to be drawing to a close, although, as Constans points out, whole speeches from other personifications could also have been left out.
1070: Hypermetric. Constans expunctuates *ad*.
1072: Hypometric. Constans: *a[m]b[e]*.
1086: Constans and Jones prefer to place the lacuna before this line. This is no doubt influenced by their decision to read *tan ha* (l. 1087) as *tanha*. As the talk is of mouths either side of the lacuna (wherever it is placed), it is probably only one verse long.
1087: *que tan ha d'onor*. Constans follows Chabaneau's suggestion to emend to *que[m] tanha donar*. See also note to l. 1086.
1101: *le*. See note to l. 86.
1120: This line seems extremely corrupt, with possible dittographies of both *mi don*, from l. 1118, and *de vos*, from l. 1121.
1127: Constans (1881) originally corrected to *Eu soi*, but then (1882) followed Chabaneau's suggestion of *Ja soi*. He misreads the start of the line as *flors*, and corrects to *Honors*.
1132: *el*: see note to l. 215. *ve(i)*: see note to l. 38.
1142: *paron*. Constans emends to *par[l]on*, no doubt by analogy with l. 1144.
1145: *devont*. See note to l. 46.
1185: Constans places the lacuna before this verse.
1186: *residada*. Constans misreads *desidada*.
1188: Hypermetric. Constans expunctuates *Dieus*.

Notes 153

1194: *amis*. This is a gallicism.
1195: *servida*. See note to l. 924. One might expect the past participle to be masculine here, as *us* is the direct object, referring to the lover.
1198: *savis*. This may well be a dittography (cf. l. 1199). Constans, following Chabaneau, corrects to *segur*. In fact, as in l. 1199, Constans and Jones misread *sains*.
1213: *ez amen*. First person plural -*n* for -*m* is rare, but not unknown (cf. l. 974). Constans prefers to correct. A scribe may have incorrectly expanded an abbreviation in a previous copy.
1217: *no·us*. Constans: *Vous. genchida*. Levy suggests correcting: *jauzida* (= *jouissance*)?
1226: *autre*. Constans corrects to *autra*. It is perhaps meant in a more neutral sense 'no other thing', or it could be another gallicism.
1228: *Ious*, 'Joy'. See Glossary. In this instance, the form may have been influenced by the sense of *iug[n]irent. si iug[n]irent*. Constans, following Chabaneau, corrects to *sian girent*.
1234: Chabaneau and Jones prefer *baisem nous en, qar conve. nous* is a gallicism.
1240: Constans follows Chabaneau in correcting to *tant abhoras adobe ssi*.
1248: *ve(i)*. See note to l. 38.
1250: Hypometric. Constans: *Que anc*. Another possibility would be *no l'[a] veges*.
1253: *nouris*. This is a gallicism.
1259: Constans describes the small superscript *r(/c?)* simply as 'un sigle' in his note to this line and corrects to *par que n'es villans*, but cannot make any sense of the passage and postulates a lacuna of two verses after this verse. He forgets, however, to include this lacuna in his line numbering. This verse is hypermetric once the *r* has been added (and nonsensical without it). This could be corrected by expunctuating the *de* at the start of the line—there is a possible dittography of the letter sequence *des* from l. 1258. As with ll. 1256–7, the sense is that love and the agency of the noble lady improve the qualities of any man. This question of the inherence of qualities in individuals is one of the key questions at issue in personification.
1262: *ch(i)ausiment*. Constans misreads *chiausimen*; Jones *chausiment*. This word has three syllables.
1266: *cill qe l'ama*. Constans gives *cill qu'el ama*, but *cill* can only be subject case (Anglade, 241).
1269: *lou*. i.e. *loc*. This is a gallicism.
1281: *eu pert*. Constans and Jones misread *en pert*. Constans places a question mark after *pert* to indicate his incomprehension.
1312: Hypermetric. Constans: *merce·us clama*.
1313: Constans corrects *Que (per) vos lo ten[ez] en gra[n]s fers*.
1314: Hypometric. Constans misreads (?) *sera el fors*.

1322: *se* . . . For the use of *se* in independent optative clauses, see Jensen, 248.
1325: Constans maintains the MS lesson *cors*, but gives no indication of what might be meant here.
1327: *scemblava un an.* Jones misreads *scemblan a un an.*
1332: The missing initial here could have been a P^s. This would make the line hypermetric, although the *ja* could easily be expunctuated. Constans's and Jones's reading ([*E*]*nasi*), whilst fitting the sense, is a long way from the lesson of the MS (although they do not acknowledge it as such).
1341: *nuailos*. The MS is smudged in this place and the *-il-* may originally have been *-ll-*. Constans certainly reads *nuallos*, whilst Jones reads *nuailos* and corrects to *nuallos*. Although *nuallos* is a more common spelling, *il* for a liquid *l* is quite normal.
1343: *avetura* may well be a dittography, as it is unusual to find a word rhymed with itself (cf. l. 1342), and this is certainly the only example in our text, but I have not been able to find an alternative rhyming word which makes better sense. Possibly the rhyming of *aventura* with *bon'avetura* was considered legitimate (for *bon'aventura* as a semantic whole, cf. *PSW*, i. 110). The line seems to be corrupt anyway in a number of respects. Constans corrects to *Un*[*s*] *drutz, en q'er bon'ave*[*n*]*tura*, but this seems awkward ('a lover in whom will be good fortune'?). More likely is that at some point a scribe missed an apostrophe indicating an abbreviation on *enqer'* (giving *enqerre*) and a later scribe added the (ungrammatically inflected) *un* to make up the missing syllable.
1346: *joiousa*. See the Glossary for *ious*. This line is hypermetric and seems corrupt. Constans prefers to expunctuate *ez* rather than *er*.
1358: *ins aisi on*. Constans, following Chabaneau, corrects to *Enaisi con* ('just as'), which is certainly clearer.
1359: This line seems very corrupt. Chabaneau suggests *si fasatz qu'eu nos* (= *no vos*) *o encus*, which Constans follows except for maintaining *u* ('prononcez *ou* = *hoc* latin'). But Constans had misread *uos* as *nos*. Taking *uencus* to be *nencus* (another case of sloppy minims in this text?), possible after the correct reading of *uos*, I arrive at the same solution in a slightly different manner.
1362: Hypermetric. Constans: *non* (*es*)*devenc*.
1367–8: These two lines do rhyme, as *ermita* is stressed on the last syllable (cf. *PSW*, iii. 126). Constans, without proposing a lacuna, rather curiously emends to *ermita*[*tje*], so that l. 1368 rhymes with the two following lines.
1369: Hypometric. Constans: *Vos es be* [*om*] *d'aquel linatje*.
1370: Hypometric. Constans: *Don son li fol drut e·l savatje*.
1378: *potra*. Another gallicism, the Occitan future form being *porra*.
1383: Constans: *Tro ques avenga es eschaia*.
1385: Hypermetric. Chabaneau suggests expunctuating either *E* or *tan*; Constans chooses the former of these options.

Notes 155

1407: Constans does not expunctuate the *u* in *lous*, but feels it necessary to follow it with an editorial *sic*. Jones omits *del mon*.

1408: *baiszares*. Although *bauzar* has the same etymology as *baisar* (cf. *FEW*, i. 269), it usually means 'tromper' (*PD*, 44), which is quite inappropriate here.

1418: There is no break in the rhyme here, but the sense (if not the syntax) seems to require that something has been left out between this line and l. 1419. Constans does not attribute a line number to this lacuna.

1423: Presumably Constans takes *sabia* to have only two syllables, as he emends: *quant [el] es*.

1430: This line has eight syllables if *E·uz* constitutes two. Constans, however, emends *metrai [a] aisz*.

1431: *progarai*. The usual form is *pregarai*. This may be another gallicism (cf. OF *proier*).

1432: *vos* (MS *uo'*). Constans expands to *von*, but the comma over the *o* usually indicates an *-s*.

1439: On *i* for *li*, see note to l. 526.

1448: Constans misreads *C'aquesta* which leads him to emend *m[i] fai*.

1450: Hypometric. Constans emends *l'uel [un] dart*.

1458: Constans does not have this line and so suggests a lacuna.

1460: Hypometric. Constans: *girofla lo cor*.

1463: Constans, following Chabaneau, marks a lacuna between ll. 1462 and 1463. He does not close the reported speech of the lover until the end of l. 1463, so he must assume that the lover moves from speaking to his messenger to apostrophizing his lady in what is missing.

1476: Constans gives *q'el sai*.

1479: *rep[re]szas*. This is no doubt simply a missed abbreviation.

1488: *si ...* See note to l. 1322.

1489: *me soi*. Constans, following Chabaneau, emends to *me sai*.

1491: Hypometric. Even if *parenta* were correct, it would not rhyme with *genta* in l. 1492 as this would mix a masculine with a feminine rhyme, so there must be at least two lines missing. The line immediately following l. 1491 may well have contained a *declinatio* of *lial* (l. 1490), such as **adoncs ai eu gran lialtat*.

1493: Hypermetric, and the imperfect seems inappropriate.

1498: Constans: *si vos (nos) o veiziatz*.

1500: Constans, following Chabaneau, emends to: *diriatz pro: "Deu[s] m'ajuda..."*. *por* (for *per*) is a gallicism (cf. l. 896).

1507: Constans misreads *E vengan ou*.

1511: *vostra*. The MS lesson could be a gallicism (*vostre* as a feminine form), but the declination is impeccable elsewhere in the text, and there are many examples of *vostra* (ll. 255, 777, 881, 921, 945 and so on).

1513: Hypometric. Constans: *soi [eu] mescrezuda*.

156 Notes

1515: Constans: *so qens taing.*
1518: Constans does not get the reference and corrects *Amats lo, mais c'aja band ric.* Although various characters called Aia and Landric are to be found in many medieval texts, no surviving work relates a love story between an Aia and a Landric. That such a tale existed and told of a great love, however, is attested in two troubadour lyrics: Pons de Capdeulh, 'Humils e francs e fis soplei vas vos', l. 42: 'Et am vos mais que Landrics no fes Aja' (Max von Napolski, *Leben und Werke des Trobadors Ponz de Capduoill* (Halle: Niemeyer, 1879), 70–2 (72)), and Peire Raimon de Tolosa, 'Ar ai ben d'amor apres', ll. 30–2: 'Qu'ieu serai de bon celar / E plus fis, si Dieus m'ampar, / Que no fo Landricx a N'Aya' (Alfredo Cavaliere, *Le poesie di Peire Raimon de Tolosa* (Florence: Olschki, 1935), 6–11 (7)). A further possible reference is in Paulet de Marselha, 'Belha dompna plazens: Ay!', ll. 3–4 (Isabel de Riquer, 'Las poesías del trovador Paulet de Marselha', *Boletín de la Real Academia de Buenas Letras de Barcelona* 38 (1979–82), 133–205 (193–6)) which actually speaks of Aya and Enricx (see the note by Isabel de Riquer, p. 195).
1522: *es soclamada. Es* is an unusual second-person plural form (see Anglade 314), also used in l. 1545. See also note to l. 1523.
1523: Constans misreads *frons no vos gieta.* Although we associate being feverish with giving off a lot of heat, the implication is that the lady's forehead is hot *because* it cannot emit heat. This is what Hippocrates calls 'ardent fever': 'on the outside he becomes cold, but inside he is hot' (*Affections*, no. 11, in *Hippocrates*, v, ed. Paul Potter, Loeb Classical Library (Cambridge, MA: Harvard University Press, 1988), 21–2).
1531: Constans and Jones: *presenteira.* In the MS, there is a small *z* inserted between the *s* and the subsequent *e.*
1533: Constans misreads and emends *C'on pus* [*vos*] *serez.*
1535: Constans, following Chabaneau, corrects *laises ges fadiar.* Jones misreads *ges famar.*
1544: Hypometric. Constans, following Chabaneau, curiously gives *mais* [*non*] *vengan.* Presumably they do not recognize *venga* as a form of *venir. ja* would surely be a better addition in that place.
1559: Constans capitalizes *Fin'Amor*, i.e. 'judged fitting by Fin'Amor'?
1560: *puis.* This is a gallicism.
1563: Hypermetric. Constans expunctuates *un.* Chabaneau proposes (*a*) instead.
1569: Constans emends *tug cil q'ho*[*m*] *demanda.* Jones misreads *tug.*
1586: *sei.* Constans corrects to *sol.*
1588: *baiszadas.* Constans corrects to *bailladas.*
1590: Constans gives *fai re*, then indicates incomprehension with a question mark at the end of the line. Syntactically, he joins l. 1591 to 1592 instead of 1590.
1595: *denier.* Constans misreads *d'amor.*
1614: Hypermetric. Constans: *Ben es fers e plens de fel(o)nia.*

1622: *fant.* See note to l. 46.
1635–42: The syntax is convoluted in this sentence. Lines 1637–8 are in apposition to each other and paranthetical to *s'Orguels non sap...qe za non er longa sazons...* (ll. 1636 and 1639).
1642: The peculiar spacing and punctuation in the MS perhaps reflect the scribe's uncertainty over this line. The only way I can make sense of *ab un oil* is to take it as qualifying the *gonfanons* in l. 1640. The peacock eye was a common emblem in medieval heraldry. Given the current state of knowledge of heraldry, especially as early as the twelfth century, I have not been able to ascertain what, if any, reference is being made with this emblem. The apparel of Honor, Valor and Baillessa d'Amor—white silk robes embroidered with gold flowers and crowns of violets (ll. 1068–73)—may also have heraldic significance. Further research in this area may help both to date and to locate the geographical production of this text.
1655: Constans and Jones place the lacuna before, rather than after, this line, but there is a change in subject from plural *ill* here to singular *el* in l. 1656.
1662: Constans corrects *bruit* to *bruida*, presumably because of *la. bruit* is attested, but masculine (see Glossary), so we must read *la* as an adverb of place.
1663: *fa·n.* Constans corrects to *fai.*
1669: Hypermetric. Constans expunctuates *de*.
1671: Constans: *si es si dons.*
1676: Constans, with some unease judging by a strategically placed question mark, follows Chabaneau's suggested correction of *falz semblantz*, although not capitalizing as Chabaneau does. If this correction is accepted, a knowledge of the *Roman de la Rose* might be imputed to the author of this text, but given that this is an isolated (and artificial) case, not supported by any other major textual parallels, and given that Fals Semblant in the *Roman de la Rose* works *for* Amor's benefit, it would be more prudent not to draw any conclusions on this basis. Constans gives *a ment* in place of *a nient*.
1683: *malparler* is obviously a plural noun here (cf. ll. 1682 and 1684). This is an interesting move from the personification to the individuals he represents. Constans capitalizes again here, but does not account for the plural verb form or for *lor*.
1687: *brut.* Constans corrects to *drut.*
1693: Constans emends *fai*[*z*], i.e. 'and now deal with your business!'
1702: *q'er.* Constans corrects to *qei* (= *que i*).
1711: *l'uel*[*s*]. . . *plor.* This collective use of (singular) eye is quite common (Jensen, 60).
1712: *manasas.* i.e. *menasas.* This is a gallicism.
1720: Hypermetric. Although we cannot know what followed l. 1721, *sor* creates a number of syntactic problems which suggest it is a mistake.

GLOSSARY

❖

This Glossary is at least partly conjectural. In a text like the *Cort d'Amor*, which only exists in one manuscript, contains frequent gallicisms and (given the frequently irregular scansion) seems to have been carelessly copied on one if not several occasions by scribes who were not native speakers of Occitan, it is hard to distinguish a rare word or form from a gallicism or a simple slip of the quill. The Glossary is divided into two parts. In the first, I have included only words which are Occitan in form, which do not appear in *PD*, and whose rare forms are either in line with the rules of etymology or to be given special credence by their presence at the rhyme. In the second part, I list all features of the text which may be classed as gallicisms. This section includes morphological features, and common Old French words are listed without comment. Words which are the result of my emendation of the manuscript are shown in italic bold print. An [r] after a line number indicates that the word occurs at the rhyme.

I. Occitan Forms

ande *adv.* (l. 1142) 'rather'. From Latin *ante*, *antea*. More commonly found as *ant*, *ans*, *anz*, in Occitan. This may simply be a contribution from the Italian scribe.

areser *v. tr./intr.?* (l. 1642) 'To mock / to arm oneself, draw up for battle'? Raynouard (ii. 118) has *aresar*, 'moquer, ridiculiser', whilst Levy (*PD*, 28) gives *arezar*, 'préparer, ajuster, équiper, disposer'. Both are possible in this context, depending on whether one takes *dec lam* to be dative or accusative.

assaiar *n. m.* (l. 501 [r]) 'the act of putting, or being put to the test' (hapax). The verb *assaiar* 'to put to the test' (cf. Raynouard, iii. 193; *PSW*, iii. 131) is here substantivized. Whereas the noun *assai* denotes the test itself, *l'assaiar* is the putting, or being put to the test. On the passive use of infinitives, see Jensen, 217–18.

bastarsa *adj.* (l. 395 [r]) 'illegitimate' (hapax). Usually *bastarda*, but cf. *FEW*, i. 276, who cites an old Dauphinois form *batars*.

bruit *n. m.* (l. 1662) 'gossip' (cf. Raynouard, ii. 265).
causida: a causida *adv.* (l. 505 [r]) 'amicably' (/'judiciously'?). *PSW* (i. 231) suggests 'in freundlicher Weise' from *cauzit*, 'nachsichtig, gütig, freundlich'. Alternatively, perhaps *a causida* is related to *cauzir*, 'voir, discerner; distinguer; choisir' (*PD*, 72) and should be translated 'judiciously'. Either makes sense here.
cimblos *n. m.* (l. 888) 'cymbal' (hapax). *PSW* (i. 254) cites this form as an alternative to *cembol*, although this poem is his only authority, and he questions whether it should not be corrected to *cimbols*.
compaina (/**compaigna**) *n. f.* (ll. 301, 1394 [r]) 'company, companionship'. This unusual form rhymes with *estraigna* (l. 1393), and on both occasions appears in conjunction with the adjective *dousa*. Elsewhere, we find the more usual form *compania* (ll. 153, 192, 193, 825), which has one syllable more.
derer: al derer *adv.* (l. 1691) 'in the end' (cf. Raynouard, v. 79, *al en derrier*; *PSW*, ii. 109, *a derier*). Cf. also *al/a premier* (*PD*, 307–8).
enia *adj.* (*f.*) (l. 206 [r]) 'annoyed, irritated' (hapax). More usually *enica*.
escarnar *v. tr.* (l. 237 [r]) 'to mock' (hapax). *PSW*, iii. 145, cites the MS form (*escanara*) and suggests correcting to *escarnira* from *escarnar* 'écharner' (cf. *PD*, 160), but this makes poor sense in this context. However, *PD* also cites *escarn* (*n. m.*) 'moquerie, raillerie, dérision; plaisanterie, mauvaise plaisanterie; ignominie, honte?', which, made into a verb, works very well in this context.
estuchat *past p.* (l. 752 [r]) from *estujar* v. tr. 'to take something away' (cf. *PSW*, iii. 358).
fait: e fait *adv.* (l. 716 [r]) 'in fact'. *PSW* (iii. 367–8) gives *metre en fach* 'als Thatsache anführen'.
garoflar *v. tr.* (l. 1460) 'to perfume'. More commonly *giroflar*, but etymologically plausible, stemming from Latin *caryophillum* (cf. Raynouard, iii. 432).
gin *n. m.* (l. 1610) 'sign, gesture, nod of the head', **faire un gin** (l. 1563 [r]) 'to give a sign, make a gesture' (cf. *guinhar* (Raynouard, iii. 520; *PSW*, iv. 215)).
ie *adv.* (l. 599) 'there'. This form stems from Latin *ibi*, via *ii* and *iei* (cf. Anglade, 70).
ious *n. m.* (ll. 1228, 1252, 1344 (?), 1463 (?)), 'joy', **joiousa** *adj.* (l. 1346 [r],) 'joyful'. *ious* usually means 'yoke', but is used as an alternative form to *ioi* in this text. In l. 1618, indeed, it makes more sense to take it to mean 'yoke'; in ll. 1344 and 1463 it could easily be either 'yoke' or 'joy'; in the other cases it certainly means 'joy'.
lam *adj.* (l. 1642) 'imperfect'? *PD* (221) is unsure about this adjective. Here too the line is not sufficiently clear to draw any definitive conclusions.

GLOSSARY 161

malan *n. m.* (l. 1398 [r]) 'wickedness' (hapax). Usually *malanha* (cf. *FEW*, under *malus* (vi. 1, 123–8)), but cf. Adams, *Word Formation* (114): as *mal* takes the suffix -*anha* only by assimilation with words deriving from Latin -*aneus* suffixes, which become either -*anh* or -*anha*, there is no *a priori* reason why it should not take -*anh*, although the other examples cited by Adams do all take -*anha*.
manti *n. m.* (l. 460) 'morning' (cf. *PSW*, v. 143).
parlan *n. m.* (l. 120 [r]) 'a place to speak' (cf. *PSW*, vi. 84, who cites one other example).
peintenat *adj.* (l. 1689) 'conceited, foppish' (cf. *PSW*, vi. 203–4).
ricedar *v. intr.* (l. 950 [r]) 'to get rich' (hapax). The usual word in Occitan for 'to become rich' is *enreqir*, as at l. 1013. Cf. *FEW*, xvi. 714, for OF *richoier*.
rodont *adj.* (l. 670 [r]) 'round'. This is more usually *redont* in Occitan, but etymologically sound as it stands (from Latin *rotondus*, cf. *FEW*, x. 519–20).
ruesa *n. f.* (l. 1261) 'rose'. This is a rare form which also occurs in Girart de Rousillon (cf. *FEW*, x. 477). Elsewhere in the text we find **rosa** (ll. 600 [r], 1627), **ruosas** (l. 56), **roza** (l. 959) and **ruesza** (l. 1601). I also correct *idesa* (l. 50) to *ruesa*, on which see the note to that line.
soclamada *adj.* (l. 1522 [r]) 'feverish' (hapax). Constans suggests *soclamada* is derived from *subclamata* 'qui se plaint' and from the context would here seem to mean 'qui a le délire de la fièvre'.
soleals *n. m.* (l. 934) 'sun'. This form is unusual (cf. *FEW*, xii. 26, which lists it as a Wallon form).
sospe *n. f.* (l. 723) 'suspicion' (hapax). From *sospeison*. On the suffix -*on* in words derived from Latin -*icio*/-*icionis*, see Adams, *Word Formation*, 243–52, and cf. *gambais*/*gambaizon* (247), *creis*/*creison* (247), *peis*/*peison* (251).
venduda *past p.* (l. 963 [r]) 'betrayed', from *vendre* 'to sell' (cf. *PSW*, viii. 632–3). *venduda* can also simply mean 'sold' (cf. l. 264).

II. Gallicisms

aimon (l. 496).
amis (l. 1194).
deporton as a first-person plural (l. 1061).
devant (ll. 58 and 726).
doin (l. 300).
el as a third-person singular feminine pronoun (ll. 215, 755, 964 (?), 1009, 1132).
envoza (l. 54 [r]). I.e. *envoia*. This word is unattested in Occitan, but it may be a gallicism, cf. 'via' ('esvoier'), *FEW* (xiv. 375).
le as an object-case masculine definite article (ll. 86, 369, 883, 1101).
loing 'a long time' (l. 609).

lou (l. 1269).
luei (l. 1022).
manasas (l. 1712).
nes (l. 941).
nouris (l. 1253 [r]).
nous (l. 1234).
-nt for third-person plural verb forms (ll. 46, 69, 376, 1145, 1622 [r]).
por (ll. 896, 1500).
potra (l. 1378).
progarai (l. 1431).
puei (l. 1018).
puis (ll. 375, 652, 715, 1560).
soltiment (l. 359 [r]). This is an unusual form of *sotilment*. *FEW* (xii. 365) lists it as an attested thirteenth-century OF form.
terre (l. 166 [r]).
vous (ll. 463, 469).

BIBLIOGRAPHY

❖

Manuscript

Provençal Chansonnier N: Pierpont Morgan Library, New York, Manuscript M.819, filmed by the Pierpont Morgan Library, 1962, fols. 31^r–46^v.

Editions of the *Cort d'Amor*

BARTSCH, KARL, *Provenzalisches Lesebuch* (Elberfeld: Friderichs, 1855), 34–8.
CHABANEAU, CAMILLE, 'Corrections', *Revue des langues romanes* 21 (1882), 90–8.
CONSTANS, LÉOPOLD, 'La cour d'Amour', *Revue des langues romanes* 20 (1881), 121–79, 209–20, 261–76.
—— *Les Manuscrits provençaux de Cheltenham (Angleterre)* (Paris: Maisonneuve, 1882), 66–115.
JONES, LOWANNE E., *The 'Cort d'Amor': A Thirteenth-Century Allegorical Art of Love*, North Carolina Studies in the Romance Languages and Literatures 185 (Chapel Hill: University of North Carolina Press, 1977).
LAVAUD, RENÉ, and NELLI, RENÉ, *Les Troubadours*, 2 vols. (Bruges: Desclée de Brouwer, 1960–6), ii. 236–43.
LEVY, EMIL, 'Corrections', *Revue des langues romanes* 21 (1882), 238–9.
MAHN, C. A. F., *Gedichte der Troubadours*, 6 vols. (Berlin: Duemmler, 1856), ii. 168–71.

Other Medieval and Classical Editions

AESOP, *Fables*, trans. Olivia and Robert Temple, Penguin Classics (Harmondsworth: Penguin, 1998).
Altercatio Phyllidis et florae, ed. Patrick Gerard Walsh, in *Love Lyrics from the Carmina Burana* (Chapel Hill: University of North Carolina Press, 1993), 101–10.
ANDREAS CAPELLANUS, *De Amore*, ed. Patrick Gerard Walsh, in *Andreas Capellanus on Love*, Duckworth Classical, Medieval and Renaissance Editions (London: Duckworth, 1982).
ARTEMIDORUS, *Oneirocritica*, ed. and trans. Robert J. White, in *The Interpretation of Dreams: 'Oneirocritica' by Artemidorus* (Park Ridge, NJ: Noyes, 1975).

Fablel dou Dieu d'Amors (Le), ed. Irville Charles Lecompte, in 'Le Fablel dou Dieu d'Amors', *Modern Philology* 8 (1910), 63–86.
GARIN LO BRUN, *Ensenhamen alla domna*, ed. Giuseppe E. Sansone, in *Testi didattico-cortesi di Provenza* (Bari: Adriatica, 1977).
HIPPOCRATES, *Affections*, ed. Paul Potter, in *Hippocrates*, vol. v., Loeb Classical Library (Cambridge, MA: Harvard University Press, 1988).
PAULET DE MARSELHA, 'Las poesias del trovador Paulet de Marselha', ed. Isabel de Riquer, *Boletín de la Real Academia de Buenas Letras de Barcelona* 38 (1979–82), 133–205.
PEIRE RAIMON DE TOLOSA, *Le poesie di Peire Raimon de Tolosa*, ed. Alfredo Cavaliere (Florence: Olschki, 1935).
PONZ DE CAPDUOILL, *Leben und Werke des Trobadors Ponz de Capduoill*, ed. Max von Napolski (Halle: Niemeyer, 1879).
Roman de la Rose (Le), ed. Daniel Poirion (Paris: Garnier Flammarion, 1974).
Venus la Déesse d'Amour (De), ed. Wendelin Foerster, in *De Venus la Déesse d'Amour: Altfranzösisches Minnegedicht aus dem XIII. Jahrhundert* (Bonn: Cohen, 1880).

Other Studies

ADAMS, EDWARD LARRABEE, *Word Formation in Provençal*, University of Michigan Studies, Humanistic Studies 2 (New York: Macmillan, 1913).
ANGLADE, JOSEPH, 'Pour l'histoire du chansonnier provençal N', *Romania* 53 (1927), 225.
AVALLE, D'ARCO SILVIO, *I manoscritti della letteratura in lingua d'oc*, new edn, rev. L. Leonardi (Turin: Einaudi, 1993).
AVRIL, FRANÇOIS, et al. (eds.), *Manuscrits enluminés d'origine italienne*, 2 vols. (Paris: Bibliothèque nationale, Département des manuscrits, 1980–4), ii: *XIIIe siècle*, ed. François Avril and M. T. Gousset, with C. Rabel.
BARDELL, MATTHEW, 'The Emergence of Narrative Secular Allegory in Old French and Occitan before 1273', Ph.D. thesis (Cambridge, 1999).
BAUMGARTNER, EMMANUÈLE, 'Le roman aux XIIe et XIIIe siècles dans la littérature occitane', in *Grundriss der romanischen Literaturen des Mittelalters*, ed. Hans Robert Jauss and Erich Köhler, 13 vols. (Heidelberg: Winter, 1968–72), IV/i. 627–44.
BRUNEL, CLOVIS FÉLIX, *Bibliographie des manuscrits littéraires en Ancien Provençal*, Société de Publications romanes et françaises 13 (Paris: Société de Publications romanes et françaises, 1935; repr. Geneva: Slatkine; Marseille: Laffitte, 1973).
BÜHLER, CURT FERDINAND, 'The Phillips Manuscript of Provençal poetry now Ms. 819 of the Pierpont Morgan Library', *Speculum* 22 (1947), 68–74.
BURE, J. J. DE, and BURE, M. J. DE, *Catalogue des livres rares et précieux de la bibliothèque de feu M. le comte de Mac-Carthy Reagh* (Paris: Crapelet, 1815), no. 2809.

Catalogus librorum manuscriptorum in bibliotheca D. Thomae Phillips (Middle Hill: [n.pub.], 1837), no. 8335.

CONSTANS, LÉOPOLD, 'Le songe vert', *Romania* 33 (1904), 490–539.

DAMMANN, O., *Die allegorische Canzone des Guiraut de Calanso 'A lieis cui am de cor e de saber' und ihre Deutung* (Breslau: Koebner, 1891).

DEGENHART, BERNHARD, and SCHMITT, ANNEGRIT, *Corpus der Italienischen Zeichnungen, 1300–1450. II: Venedig; Addenda zu Süd- und Mittelitalien,* i: *Katalog 636–664: Venedig 1300–1400* (Berlin: Mann, 1980).

FARAL, EDMOND, *Recherches sur les sources latines des contes et romans courtois du moyen âge* (Paris: Champion, 1913).

FOLENA, GIANFRANCO, 'Tradizione e cultura trobadorica nelle corti e nelle città venete', in *Storia della cultura veneta* (Vicenza: Neri Pozza, 1976), 453–562.

FRASSO, GIUSEPPE, 'Petrarca, Andrea da Mantova e il canzoniere provenzale N', *Italia medioevale e umanistica* 17 (1974), 185–205.

GAUNT, SIMON, 'Bel Acueil and the improper allegory of the *Romance of the Rose*', *New Medieval Literatures* 2 (1998), 65–93.

GUNN, ALAN MURRAY FINLAY, *The Mirror of Love* (Lubbock: Texas Tech, 1952).

HARRSEN, META, and BOYCE, GEORGE K., *Italian Manuscripts in the Pierpont Morgan Library* (New York: Pierpont Morgan Library, 1953).

HENTSCH, ALICE ADÈLE, *De la littérature didactique du moyen âge s'adressant spécialement aux femmes* (Cahors: Couselant, 1903).

HULT, DAVID F., *Self-fulfilling Prophecies: Readership and Authority in the First 'Roman de la Rose'* (Cambridge: Cambridge University Press, 1986).

HUOT, SYLVIA, *From Song to Book: The Poetics of Writing in Old French Lyric and Narrative Poetry* (Ithaca: Cornell University Press, 1987).

—— *The Romance of the Rose and its Medieval Readers: Interpretation, Reception, Manuscript Transmission* (Cambridge: Cambridge University Press, 1993).

JAUSS, HANS ROBERT, 'Theorie der Gattungen und Literatur des Mittelalters', in *Grundriss der romanischen Literaturen des Mittelalters*, ed. Hans Robert Jauss and Erich Köhler, 13 vols. (Heidelberg: Winter, 1968–72), i. 107–38.

JEANROY, ALFRED, *Bibliographie sommaire des chansonniers provençaux* (Paris: Champion, 1916).

—— *Histoire sommaire de la poésie occitane des origines à la fin du XVIIIe siècle* (Toulouse: Privat, 1945).

JONES, LOWANNE E., '*Lo Saber* dans les quatre allégories occitanes du XIIIe siècle', in *Studia Occitanica in memoriam Paul Remy*, ed. H.-E. Keller, 2 vols. (Kalamazoo: Michigan Medieval Institute, 1986), ii. 81–92.

—— 'Narrative transformations of twelfth-century troubadour lyric', in *The Expansions and Transformations of Courtly Literature: Selected Papers from the Second Triennial Congress of the International Courtly Literature Society*, ed. N. B. Smith and J. T. Snow (Athens: Georgia University Press, 1980), 117–27.

Bibliography

JUNG, MARC-RENÉ, *Etudes sur le poème allégorique en France au moyen âge*, Romanica Helvetica 82 (Bern: Franke, 1971).

KAY, SARAH, *Subjectivity in Troubadour Poetry* (Cambridge: Cambridge University Press, 1990).

KELLY, DOUGLAS, *The Art of Medieval French Romance* (Madison: University of Wisconsin Press, 1992).

—— *Internal Difference and Meanings in the 'Roman de la Rose'* (Madison: University of Wisconsin Press, 1995).

LAFITTE-HOUSSAT, JACQUES, *Troubadours et cours d'amour* (Paris: Presses Universitaires de France, 1950).

LAFONT, ROBERT, and ANATOLE, CHRISTIAN, *Nouvelle Histoire de la littérature occitane*, Publications de l'institut d'études occitanes, 2 vols. (Bruges: Presses Universitaires de France, 1960–6).

LANGLOIS, ERNEST, *Les Manuscrits du 'Roman de la Rose': description et classement*, Travaux et mémoires de l'université de Lille, Nouvelle série i. Droit–lettres 7 (Lille: Tallandier; Paris: Champion, 1910).

—— *Origines et sources du Roman de la Rose*, Bibliothèque des Ecoles françaises d'Athènes et de Rome (Paris: Thorin, 1890).

LOOMIS, ROBERT SHERMAN, and LOOMIS, LAURA HIBBARD, *Arthurian Legends in Medieval Art*, Modern Language Association of America Monograph Series 9 (New York: Modern Language Association of America, 1938; repr. New York: Kraus Reprint, 1975).

MEYER, PAUL, 'Les troisièmes personnes du pluriel en provençal', *Romania* 9 (1883), 192–215.

—— 'L'imparfait du subjonctif en *es*', *Romania* 8 (1879), 155–62.

MONSON, DON A., *Les 'Ensenhamens' occitans: essai de définition et de délimitation du genre* (Paris: Klincksieck; Geneva: Droz, 1981).

MÜLLER, ERICH, *Die altprovenzalische versnovelle* (Halle: Niemeyer, 1930).

NEILSON, WILLIAM ALLAN, *The Origins and Sources of the Court of Love*, Studies and Notes in Philology and Literature 6 (Boston: Ginn, 1899).

OULMONT, CHARLES, *Les Débats du clerc et du chevalier dans la littérature poétique du moyen âge* (Paris: Champion, 1911).

PARDUCCI, AMOS, *Costumi ornati: studi sugli insegnamenti di cortigiania medievali* (Bologna: Zanichelli, 1927).

PATERSON, LINDA, 'Review of Lowanne E. Jones, *The 'Cort d'Amor''*, *French Studies* 35 (1981), 425.

PILLET, ALFRED, and CARSTENS, HENRY, *Bibliographie der Troubadours*, Schriften der Königsberger Gelehrten Gesellschaft, Sonderreihe 3 (Halle: Niemeyer, 1933; repr. New York: Franklin, 1968).

REMY, PAUL, 'Les "cours d'amour": légende et réalité', *Revue de l'université de Bruxelles* 7 (1954–5), 179–97.

STIMMING, ALBERT, 'Provenzalische Literatur', in *Grundriss der romanischen Philologie*, ed. Gustav Gröber, 2 vols. (Strassburg: Trübner, 1888–1902), ii. 1–69.

SUCHIER, HERMANN, 'Il canzoniere provenzale di Cheltenham', *Rivista di filologia romanza* 2 (1875), 49–52, 144–72.

TAYLOR, ROBERT, 'The figure of *Amor* in the Old Provençal narrative allegories', in *Court and Poet: Proceedings of the Third Congress of the International Courtly Literature Society*, ed. G. S. Burgess *et al.* (Liverpool: Cairns, 1980), 309–17.

ZUFFEREY, FRANÇOIS, *Recherches linguistiques sur les chansonniers provençaux*, Publications romanes et françaises 176 (Geneva: Droz, 1987).

ZUMTHOR, PAUL, *Essai de poétique médiévale* (Paris: Seuil, 1972).

INDEX

❖

Aia et Landric 156
Aimeric de Peguillan, 'Qui la vi, en ditz' 39
alba 8, 23
allegorical romance 5, 12, 28
allegory 8, 9, 10, 16, 19–28
Altercatio Phyllidis et Florae 31 n. 43
Amenieu de Sescas 8
Amor 14, 16–25
   army of 13
   fire of 21, 26
   garden of 3
   gender of 8, 9, 14–15, 31 n. 38, 37
amplificatio 23
Andreas Capellanus, *De Amore* 4–5, 13–14, 16, 32 n. 52, 139
Apuleius, *Metamorphoses* 14
Ardimen 20, 25, 27
art of love 9, 14–16
Artemidorus, *Oneirocritica* 139

Baillessa d'Amor 19, 20, 22, 27, 28
Bartolomeo Zorzi 148
Bel Acueil 33 n. 68
Bernart de Ventadorn 25
birds 25–7
Bon'Esperansa 20, 25
'Bona Dompna pros ez onrada' 39

Celamen 20, 21, 25, 26
   banner of 21
censorship 23
chansonniers
   L 29 n. 1
   N 1–2, 6, 29, 30 n. 19, 36, 39
Chrétien de Troyes, *Cligès* 143
classical gods 22
Claudian 14
Cobezesa 21

Coindia (Na) 20, 22, 149–50
Concilium Remiremontensis 31 n. 45
Cortesa d'Amor 9, 17–19, 20, 21, 22, 145
Corteszia 9, 17–19, 20, 21, 22, 27
courtly love 16–19, 22–3, 27
courts of love 7, 11–15, 23
Cupid 14

deconstruction 23, 24–5, 28
Deport 19, 20, 21–2, 149–50
dialogue 9, 10, 13, 14, 16–19, 20, 21, 22, 23–4
   internal 141–2
didacticism 8, 9, 10, 12–13, 16, 19, 28
Dompneis 20, 22, 25
Dousa Compaina 20, 25
Drudaria 20, 23, 25

Eleanor d'Aquitaine 14
ensenhamens 8, 9, 16
epithalamia 14
Ermengarde de Narbonne 13, 14
exegesis 25

fable of ant and lion 139
Fablel dou Dieu d'Amors 11
Fals'Amor 25
Fin'Amor 27
flowers 21, 25–7
fountains 9, 21, 26
Fortuna 14

Gaibana, Giovanni 1–2, 29 n. 6
gaita, see watchman
gallicisms 3–5, 14, 35, 36–7
Garin lo Brun, *Ensenhamen alla domna* 16
Gauvain 143
gender 12–19, 25, 28

gloss 24
Gradus amoris 17, 20
Guillaume de Lorris, see *Roman de la Rose, Le*
heraldry 157
Hippocrates, *Affections* 156
Honor 19, 20, 21, 22, 25, 27
Husayn-ibn-Ishak, *see* Johannitius

Isobel de Vermandois 14

Jaufre Rudel 25
Jean de Meun 5, 22
Jean de Nostredame 11
jewellery 22
joc partit 13
Joi (Don) 17, 20
 crown of 21, 22, 25, 27
Johannitius 14, 139
jongleurs 21, 149–50
Joven 19, 20

knight and cleric debates 11

Landric, *see* Aia et Landric
Larguesza 20, 25
lausengiers 19, 20, 22, 24, 26
locus amoenus 11
lost ending 23, 39

Male Bouche 32 n. 68
manuscript illustrations 1–2
Marcoul et Salamon (Les Dits de) 151
Marie de Champagne
 court of 4, 13–14
Merce 12, 20, 21, 25, 26
messenger 19, 23
metaphor 21, 23, 25–7

nominalism 24

Orgeuil 11, 19, 20, 21, 22, 24, 27
Ovid, *Ars amatoria* 16
 Ovidian love 16, 18–19, 22–3, 27, 28

Painelli, Andrea 1
Painelli, Giacomino 1

Paor 18, 20
Parnassus 8, 17, 22
partimen 13
Paulet de Marselha, 'Belha dompna plazens: Ay!' 156
peacock eye 157
Peire Raimon de Tolosa, 'Ar ai ben d'amor apres' 156
Peire Vidal 25
personification 11, 18, 19–28, 37
 gender of 14–15, 25, 37
Plaser 19, 20
Pons de Capdeulh, 'Humils e francs e fis soplei vas vos' 156
Pret Z20
Proessa 19, 20, 21, 22, 23, 24, 25, 27
Psyche 14
psychomachia 8, 20

realism (philosophical) 24, 25, 27
Ris 19, 20, 21–2, 23, 149–50
Roman de la Rose, Le 3, 5, 7, 12, 16, 20, 22, 24, 25, 27, 157
roses 26

Salamon, see *Marcoul et Salamon*
semantic shading 21, 28
Sens 19, 20, 22
Sidonius 14
Solaz (Don) 17, 20, 26
Songe vert, Le 7
Soredamors 143
syllepsis 25

tenso 13
troubadours 3, 14, 25

universals 19, 24–5, 27, 32 n. 66

Valor 19, 20, 21, 22, 23, 28
Venus 14
Vénus, la Déesse d'Amor, (De) 11
Vérité 32 n. 68
Vilania 11, 25
voicing 23

watchman 8, 21, 23

SOCIETY FOR FRENCH STUDIES

The Society for French Studies, the oldest and leading learned association for French studies in the UK and Ireland, promotes teaching and research in French studies in higher education. Membership is open to all interested; postgraduates and lecturers in the first three years of employment pay a reduced subscription. The Society's activities include:

- Editing *French Studies*, a quarterly journal (articles in French literary and cultural studies and a wide range of book reviews) and its companion *French Studies Bulletin* (short articles, information from societies, calls for papers, etc.), both sent free to members

- Maintaining the online database of research projects in the UK and Ireland, *Current Research in French Studies* (at www.sfs.ac.uk), and compiling the annual *Directory of Postgraduate Research Students of French*, free to members

- Hosting an annual conference with distinguished speakers and varied workshops

- Promoting research through: conference and seminar grants; the R.H. Gapper annual book and essay prizes; joint publication of Legenda Research Monographs in French Studies (with 33% discount to SFS members); postgraduate support via subsidized membership fees and conference expenses, an electronic bulletin board and other services

- Maintaining a website with rapidly expanding resources: **www.sfs.ac.uk**

Membership enquiries: Dr Catherine O'Brien
School of Languages, Kingston University, Penrhyn Road
Kingston-on-Thames KT1 2EE, UK
membership@sfs.ac.uk

The Society for French Studies is charity no. 1078038 and is a company, limited by guarantee, registered in England and Wales, no. 3801778, whose registered office is the Taylor Institution, Oxford OX1 3NA.